Sacred Secrets

ISBN: 978-1-62166-800-8

XPmedia.com

Sacred Secrets is available at store@xpmedia.com
and Amazon.com

TABLE OF CONTENTS

FOREWORD

by Patricia King

In Mark, Chapter Four, Jesus taught a crowd the story about the sower and the seed. After communicating the parable, He declared, "He who has ears to hear, let him hear." The disciples were perplexed and longed for insight. Following the teaching they asked Him for further understanding. His response was, "To you has been given the mystery of the kingdom of God, but those who are outside get everything in parables" (Mark 4:11).

At a lecture I once attended, Linguist and Bible translator Dr. Brian Simmons shared an outstanding insight on the PaRDeS[1] model of Hebrew Exegesis that goes back for nearly three-thousand years. PaRDeS is an acronym formed from the initials of the following four levels of understanding in Hebrew thought:

1. Pashot: "Plain" – That which is plainly heard, seen, or understood from the communication ... the obvious.

2. Ramez: "Hint" – Understanding that comes from a hint that is seen within the context.

---

[1] http://en.m.wikipedia.org/wiki/Pardes_(Jewish_exegesis)

3. Derash: "Inquire, seek" – Understanding that comes from inquiring, studying, going deeper

4. Sod: "Secret, mystery" – Understanding that is imparted by revelation from God

In Mark chapter four, Jesus' followers desired deeper understanding. As they sought for it and made inquiry *(Derash)*, Jesus granted them the level of understanding that comes through revelatory mystery *(Sod)*.

Shirley Seger is a woman who passionately desires the deeper understanding of the Lord and His Kingdom. She is a seer who is prophetically motivated and is known by those who are close to her as one with integrity and Christ-like character. In December of 2012, she began to daily take communion and seek the Lord from 6:00 a.m. to 7:00 a.m. As she made inquiry of the Lord, she was daily taken by the Holy Spirit into encounter and was given access into realms, insights, and mysteries of the Kingdom of God.

She carefully wrote down what the Spirit revealed. The revelations were received through a number of different means as she followed the leading of the Spirit. Sometimes she acknowledged the revelation through still, small thoughts or impressions, sometimes through Scriptures, and at other times through vivid visions, words, and sounds. She encountered the sevenfold nature of Jesus; the Spirit of the Lord, and the Spirit of Wisdom, of Understanding, of Counsel, of Might, of Knowledge and of the Fear of the LORD as well as a variety of angels and heavenly beings during these encounters.

Often, after she had the encounters, she would read to me from her journal. The presence of the Lord would fall heavy upon me as I hung on every word. Within each story were layers of revelation and insight that not only enlightened me, but also walked me through the four levels of understanding mentioned above. I found myself visited by revealed mysteries from the heart of God.

In Mark 4:33-34, the Scripture states that, "With many such parables He was speaking the word to them, so far as they were able to hear it; and He did not speak to them without a parable; but He was explaining everything privately to His own disciples."

The word "parable" comes from the Greek παραβολή (parabolē), meaning "comparison, illustration, or analogy."

Sacred Secrets is a compilation of some of Shirley's journal notes from her encounters. Some of you might simply find in each account an entertaining story or illustration that you might even equate with something fictitious, but others of you will read *Sacred Secrets* and be led into the intimate and secret place in Christ's heart, where He reveals deep mysteries and grants divine encounters in the God realm.

I love this book and everything in me calls for more of Christ as I read it – "Deep calls unto deep" (Psalm 42:7). May you, the reader, be led into depths of the realities of God's glory and Kingdom that you have never yet discovered. May you, the reader, experience sacred secrets and mysteries found in Christ.

Patricia King
Patricia King Ministries
Maricopa, Arizona
August, 2017

WHY I WROTE THIS BOOK

Ever since I can remember I just "knew" things. I didn't know how I knew them – I just did. Many times, the knowledge came through pictures in my mind, other times through visual observation, still other times it was simply an application of the knowledge I had previously received. But the one I cherished the most was the still, small voice that spoke to me about great and wonderful things.

Some called it intuition, some premonition, others psychic ability. At first, I thought this still-small-voice-within was just my own thoughts of hope, encouragement, love, patience or optimism, but over time I realized I wasn't that smart, that kind or that good. I came to welcome that voice and its leading as Wisdom's whisper, a gift from God that I believe every Christian believer has the ability to hear.

> To one there is given through the Spirit the message of wisdom,
> to another a message of knowledge by means of the same Spirit.   – 1 Corinthians 12:8 (NIV)

This book is the fruit of hours of mining God's Word for the deeper truths hidden within. Each jewel I discovered always lined up with Scripture, was timely and peaceful, and directed my mind and heart toward a righteous path of humility, forgiveness, repentance, love and charity.

I am not a theologian, ordained minister or teacher of the law of God. I'm simply a lover, believer and follower of Jesus Christ, the Son of God. What follows are my experiences with Jesus and encounters in the spirit. May your eyes be opened to the wisdom and revelation of the knowledge of the Creator and Savior of all.

 Shirley Seger has a remarkable gift of spiritual sight and discernment that began as a child. Her training as a Creative Producer in Hollywood contributes to her book's unique ability to reach the hearts of readers in a style they will never forget. Shirley has worked with and been mentored by Patricia King, James Goll, Clarice Fluitt, and others for the past 15 years. She is co-founder and CEO of XPmedia.com and produces Patricia King's long running television show "Everlasting Love." Shirley and her husband Donn reside in Maricopa, Arizona.

1

ESCORT TO HEAVEN

The fear of the Lord is the beginning of wisdom, And the knowledge of the Holy One is understanding.

— Proverbs 9:10

What happens after we die? Is there life after death? What is life in heaven like? Am I going there? What is life like in hell? Why doesn't God show Himself to us? Are blue and green God's favorite colors?

As I lay upon my bed pondering the meaning of life and my purpose in it, I asked myself, "Wouldn't it be amazing if I could make an appointment with God to ask Him all these questions face-to-face?" I squeezed my eyes shut and asked if it were possible.

Suddenly, the atmosphere in my apartment changed and I sensed a presence. In the spirit, I walked into the living room, where I saw an angel sitting on my couch flipping through a magazine. His shoulder-length hair was a blond "light" – literally, it was made of light. His eyes appeared to be entirely blue iris with no pupil and shone with golden light as if he had a spotlight inside. His garb was that of a Roman gladiator complete with a breastplate and purple "skirt." He had wings that folded around him like a coat. I was astonished at his casualness and intrigued beyond belief by the radiating hum of power he was emitting.

"Who are you?" I asked, with eyes the size of saucers.

"I am a messenger of God," he answered.

"What are you doing here?" I asked.

With evident equal curiosity toward me, he said, "You ask a lot of questions. I've been sent to give you the answer."

My mind wandered, captivated by his appearance. "You look like a glowing cartoon! Like an animation, but a bit more real," I said, half to myself, as the experience seemed like a dream.

"Are you ready to go?" the angel asked.

"Go where?" I asked.

"To get the answer to all your questions. Will you go?" he asked me.

"Yes!" I heard myself say.

As he stood up his wings unfolded and his head touched the ceiling. He extended his hand to me and as I took it, we left the room and were immediately in a waiting room, not unlike my dentist's. Other people were seated next to their angels and were quietly writing on small pieces of paper. My angel handed me a pen and paper and said, "You might want to write down your questions; many times memory fails when you stand before the King." I sat down and began to write.

Why do You remain invisible to us?

What was Your central goal in creating man?

Did You know some would turn their backs on You? If so, why did You create them?

What is heaven like and what will we do there?

Is eternity a measure of time or time forever?

Has time always been constant?

Why does prayer and the laying on of hands not always heal?

What actually happens when we die?

What are Watchers and what are they watching?

Have I ever entertained an angel unaware?

What is the cure for Parkinson's, blood disease and cancer?

What are Your plans for my life and am I on track?

I paused a moment and watched the lady next to me write only one question on her paper. Only one question – was she nuts? This was the chance of a lifetime! Maybe she just wasn't as spiritual as I was. I had pretty much filled both sides of the paper when the door opened and my name was called.

"That lady only had one question – is that all we are allowed to ask?" I whispered to my angel.

He answered, "She has been here before, so she only has one question."

His answer puzzled me as he motioned for me to follow him. My heart began to pound within me. Was I really about to come before the King of the universe?!? I had thousands of questions for Him, not just one like that lady, I thought with pride.

2

THE THRONE
OF GRACE

Enter into His gates with thanksgiving, and into His courts with praise. Be thankful to Him, and bless His name.

– Psalm 100:4 (NKJV)

This place was enormous. The length of the hallway was equal in size to the height of the ceiling. The floors radiated enormous power and I could feel every cell in my body begin to swell and grow strong with each step I took.

A line of thousands of people, escorted by angels, stretched the distance between us and the gigantic double doors ahead. Our feet tread upon a rich red carpet made of an unusually soft, almost squishy, substance. The long line didn't affect me like lines on Earth did, as it moved at the pace of a brisk walk. My body felt so alive and aligned, my mind sharp and clear.

Standing at each side of the wide-open double doors ahead were two guardian angels that stood over three-hundred-feet tall. Above the door were the words "Throne of Grace." I asked my angel, "What does 'grace' mean?" He looked at me puzzled. I added, "I know it means gracious or nice and elegant, but in terms of God, what does it mean when you say, 'grace and peace be with you'? Is grace a substance of some kind?"

Without waiting for the answer, I said to myself, "I think I'll add that question to my list." I looked up at the words Throne of Grace high above the door. "Does He have more than one throne room?"

My angel answered, "Yes, He has three. The Throne of Grace is the throne of favor and provision. It is really the only one you'll ever want to come before."

Before I could ask what the other two were called, we entered the room. Thousands upon thousands filled the room which radiated with excitement and expectation. The smell was intoxicating and the light sparkled like gemstones. Worship music rolled over us like waves of warm honey. I looked around at the others whose faces shone with love and I wondered how they could be so calm while I felt like a colt about to be released from its stall.

"Have you been here before?" I asked a woman standing beside me.

"Oh, yes, I come every day," she said matter-of-factly.

"Every day?" I asked.

She smiled and said, "We all have only one question we ask Him every day."

I felt panicked, like I hadn't been told the rules and was about to be humiliated by my paper stuffed full of questions – seeking answers I couldn't believe they wouldn't all want to know as well. "Are we only allowed to ask one question?" I asked her in a hushed tone.

Her answer was kind and gentle, "Oh, no, you may ask Him anything you desire, but there is really only one question we all want to know each day."

"You all ask the same question over and over again?" I asked a bit aghast.

She nodded with a smile, then asked me, "Would you like to know what it is?"

"Oh, yes, please!" I answered. She opened her paper and showed me the question.

3

THE REVELATION

In a moment, I completely understood the message this angel had been sent to deliver. I turned to him and said, "I'm not ready to go before Him, I'm not worthy, I want to leave!" I grabbed his hand and was instantly back in my room, on my bed, alone. My heart pounded within me and tears filled my eyes as I realized how utterly selfish, irreverent, and prideful I had been. That woman's question was a simple one in which all others are answered. One question I had never pondered or even thought to ask.

"What can I do for You today, my King of Glory?"

The revelation of my irreverent, arrogant attitude filled me with deep sorrow. The inner voice spoke gently to me, "It is okay to be curious about creation and to seek out knowledge and understanding. God delights in your curiosity and gives wisdom without measure to all who ask. But to seek the deeper things first requires 'the Fear of the Lord' – reverent respect and honor with the knowledge of His majesty and your position and destiny before Him."

"As a little child leans on their father's understanding," the voice continued, "so must you lean on your Heavenly Father's. You have asked many times for the wisdom of Solomon. You have done well. There is a wisdom greater than Solomon's that will be fully revealed to you if you continue to seek. The beginning of this wisdom is to know that His power is beyond your understanding. His mind and thoughts, higher than yours. His ways, always trustworthy and righteous. You must begin your quest for wisdom and knowledge firmly established on this foundation.

"Trust in the Lord your God with all your heart, with all your mind and with all your strength. *Lean not on your own understanding,* but in all your ways acknowledge Him and He will crown your efforts with success.

"Looks like your own understanding has garnered you very few crowns?" I heard my angel shout from my living room.

4

TEST THE SPIRITS

I leapt off my bed and marched into the living room, sat down on the coffee table and looked directly into this angel's eyes – you can see so much when you really look into someone's eyes. If you hold their gaze long enough to engage spirit to spirit, you will just know-that-you-know the nature of their true character.

> Beloved, do not believe every spirit, but test the spirits to see whether they are from God, because many false prophets have gone out into the world. By this you know the Spirit of God: every spirit that confesses that Jesus Christ has come in the flesh is from God; and every spirit that does not confess Jesus is not from God; this is the spirit of the antichrist, of which you have heard that it is coming, and now it is already in the world.
>
> – 1 John 4:1-3

I had never encountered an angel in this way before and just had to be sure my discernment about him was correct.

"Tell me who Jesus Christ is to you?" I asked.

He began without hesitation or forethought:

"Jesus Christ is the essential Word of God...

...the personal wisdom and power in union with God, His minister in creation and government of the universe,
...the cause of all the world's life, both physical and ethical,
...who – for the procurement of man's salvation – put on human nature in the person of Jesus the Messiah, the second person in the Godhead, and shone forth conspicuously from His words and deeds.

"Jesus Christ is Lord!

"The Son of the Lord God Most High was born of a virgin, bore the flesh of man,
...endured all temptations known to man, divested of powers and rights. He was condemned to death by His own people; He took thirty-nine brutal lashes from a Roman whip and crushing blows to His face and head, had His beard ripped out, was stripped naked and ridiculed,
…all so that His beloved creation – man – might be reconciled and healed.

"He personally carried your sins in His body on the cross so that you could be dead to sin and live righteous before God.

"By His wounds you were healed as He endured the agony and humiliation of the cross so that you could live a life with true peace, free of oppression from supernatural forces of evil, and walk in His power.

"His mortal body died on the cross.

"He...

... descended into hell where He paid every one of your debts and took your punishment upon Himself.

Paid it all in full,

...conquered the gates of hell and set the captives free,

...stripped the devil of all power and took the keys to death and hell,

...rose from the dead and handed His power to you and told you to do the same miracles, the same wonders He did and even greater miracles than these, in order to gather back to Him His lost beloved children.

"He is my Lord and my Master whom I was created to serve into all eternity.

"He is who I love, who I fight for and serve, who I will always defend!

"Jesus is Lord!"

The fierce adoration in his eyes released a solemn reverence into the atmosphere and caused me to weep. He loved Him, too!

"Yes," I said, "I am willing to exchange my understanding for His."

"Very well!" the angel exclaimed. "I have been sent by God to show you His original intent for creation." He stood and took a small scroll out of his pocket and began to read.

5

THE PURE LANGUAGE

"**E**vidence of a changed heart is a changed vocabulary. *Original Intent* means: The theory of interpretation by which one attempts to ascertain the meaning of creation by determining how the creation was understood at the time it was first created.

"For you to understand Adam's point of view, you must first know the pure language that existed at the time, before it was defiled and mixed with evil as your language is today," the angel explained.

> For then will I restore to the peoples a pure language, that they all may call on the name of the LORD, to serve Him with one accord.   – Zephaniah 3:9 (NKJV)

"Like a drop of ink in a bucket of pure water, your language became defiled and mixed with the knowledge of evil. In the Garden, Adam and Eve had only one teacher, God Himself. The Father taught them the knowledge of pure truth and allowed Adam to formulate his own language. Adam's interpretation of creation established its nature and fame. God created a lion and pronounced that it was 'good,' then brought the lion before Adam to decree its nature. So before a lion was called a lion, Adam saw its nature as strong and brave, heralded it as a king of beasts, gave it its name, and thus the meaning of the word 'lion' today."

> And out of the ground the LORD God formed every beast of the field, and every fowl of the air; and brought them unto Adam to see what he would call them: and whatsoever Adam called every living creature, that was the name thereof.
>
> – Genesis 2:19 (KJV)

The angel continued, "At that time, Adam's language was pure communication of truth, void of confusion and mixture ... a system of words and rules, based firmly on the will of God alone and used to create and tend the world around him. Evil was unknown and, therefore, undefined with words.

"But when Adam and Eve took upon themselves the knowledge of good and evil, they invited another teacher into the Garden, one that competed with God's holy truths. The knowledge of evil demanded definition. The formulation of words that gave name and nature to the works of evil polluted the pure language. These words directly challenged and contradicted the Word of God, giving birth to doubt."

> You are not a better judge than the Lord, or wiser than the Most High! Let many perish who are now living, rather than that the law of God that is set before them be disregarded! For the Lord strictly commanded those who came into the world, when they came, what they should do to live, and what they should observe to avoid punishment. Nevertheless they were not obedient, and spoke against him; they devised for themselves vain thoughts, and proposed to themselves wicked frauds; they even declared

that the Most High does not exist, and they ignored his ways. They scorned his law, and denied his covenants; they have been unfaithful to his statutes, and have not performed his works.

— (Apocrypha) 2 Esdras 7:19-24

"The Lord gave you an example of this event in His parable about the wheat and the weeds," explained the angel.

Jesus told them another parable: 'The kingdom of heaven is like a man who sowed good seed in his field. But while everyone was sleeping, his enemy came and sowed weeds among the wheat, and went away. When the wheat sprouted and formed heads, then the weeds also appeared.

"The owner's servants came to him and said, 'Sir, didn't you sow good seed in your field? Where then did the weeds come from?'

"'An enemy did this,' he replied.

"The servants asked him, 'Do you want us to go and pull them up?'

"'No,' he answered, 'because while you are pulling the weeds, you may uproot the wheat with them. Let both grow together until the harvest. At that time I will tell the harvesters: First collect the weeds and tie them in bundles to be burned; then gather the wheat and bring it into my barn.'"

— Matthew 13:24-30 (NIV)

The angel flipped open his book and showed me a picture of wheat and weeds together.

"You see, as they grow they look the same, but when they reach their fullness, the wheat bows but the weeds do not! The wheat bears light fruit, good to eat, but the weed's fruit is black and useless. Faith in God and belief in His ways comes through hearing the WORD(s) of God. Faith in the enemy and belief in his ways comes through hearing the contaminated words or 'weeds' planted in the garden."

> Their throat is an open sepulchre; with their tongues they have used deceit; the poison of asps is under their lips: Whose mouth is full of cursing and bitterness.   – Romans 3:13-14 (KJV)

> You shall also say to this people, "Thus says the LORD, 'Behold, I set before you the way of life and the way of death.'"
> – Jeremiah 21:8

The angel's face carried great warning, "I have watched centuries of the lives of man and I tell you this plainly, the enemy comes to the children of men dressed as an angel of light to feed them his mingled words. 'My Rights' and 'I Deserve' will blind you to the crooked path of destruction you enter. Oh, how your enemy delights in the astonished anguish of each human soul who unknowingly chooses the path of evil to the end!"

> But were mingled among the heathen, and learned their works.
> – Psalm 106:35 (KJV)

"How can we purify our language again?" I asked.

"The best way to identify a counterfeit is to become intimately familiar with the original!" He took a huge, badly worn leather-bound version of the *Oxford English Dictionary* out of a pocket under his wing and with great enthusiasm said, "I have taken the liberty of studying your dictionary's noble attempt to reveal the full meaning of all your words. The Second Edition of the twenty-volume *Oxford English Dictionary* contains full entries for 171,476 words in current use and 47,156 obsolete words. To this may be added around 9,500 derivative words included as sub-entries." He seemed lost in his own little world of exploration.

"This suggests," he continued, "that there are, at the least, a quarter of a million distinct English words, excluding inflections, and words from technical and regional vocabulary not covered by this book, or words not yet added to the published dictionary, of which perhaps 20% are no longer in current use. If distinct senses were counted, the total would probably approach three quarters of a million words in your vocabulary." He shook his head, astonished and amused. "No wonder so many of you are lost and confused!"

"Wow, so you are an intellectual angel?" I asked.

"Intellectual?" He looked up the word and read, "Intellect – having to do with the understanding of complex or abstract truths." He snapped the book closed and said, "Case in point! Complex or abstract truths? Truth is not abstract or complex, it is quite simple. And yet your dictionary, compiled to assist your understanding, defines "truth" as theoretical, complex, left to interpretation! Diabolical! Are you following with understanding?" he asked.

INTERPRETATION OF TRUTH

"How many words are in the language of angels?" I asked.

"Perhaps one tenth the number of mankind's. Our language – and yours when you speak in tongues – expresses whole truths and concepts, not just a simple piece of a theory. Rather, it encompasses the entirety of a subject as well as deep groanings for righteousness. Our words are coated in love and adhere to the Holy Word. Therefore our language is pure truth without mixture," he explained. "The sons and daughters of Adam who carry the Spirit of the Lord and speak with the language of angels release great power – the power given to you by Christ Jesus the Lord."

If I speak with the tongues of men and of angels, but do not have love, I have become a noisy gong or a clanging cymbal.

– 1 Corinthians 13:1

"This dictionary is man's definition of truth apart from God. In their original condition, Adam and Eve were clothed in God's glory, grace and power. They wholeheartedly accepted what God said was "good" and "evil" and only sought understanding, not interpretation. After the fall from Grace, man began to define their own version of truth and decided for themselves what was good and what was evil. Soon good became evil and evil, good."

Woe to those who are wise in their own eyes and clever in their own sight! – Isaiah 5:21

"Man formed many new words to communicate the laws opposed to God's absolutes!"

The angel further illustrated, "Let's say a child is told by his parent that fire is not to be taken outside the stone circle. But the child likes the heat, light and life of the fire and decides to take it to his bedroom to light his room at night. He sets the fire upon his bed and burns the house down. His desire – which was outside the stated laws established by his parent to protect him – brought about destruction. This 'choosing their own path' is the cause of all adversity, pain and death in the world today, plain and simple.

"Are you ready to meet your Lord?" he asked.

6

A HEART MAKEOVER

I stood before a huge fireplace in what felt like an ancient medieval castle. Lounging at a table was the Lord Jesus, dressed in "casual" clothing – the kind you wear at night to recline for the evening. He sipped a cup of coffee.

"Come and sit," He said. "I have your favorite here for you."

A steaming cup of coffee sat on the table with a perfect heart swirled into the cream. "There are some things you need to know about your decision today," He said to me. I sat down in awe of Him who sat so casually before me. I desperately tried to keep my mind still and sure that this was actually happening. I could feel myself lifting out of the scene as if it were beyond me why Jesus would want to sit with me.

"You must read Romans over and over to get rid of that urgency to flee, beloved," He said, with twinkling eyes. He knew my every thought, every intent, every motive of my heart – and still looked at me with those amazing eyes of love. I was stunned and remained silent.

"I will have you know the conditions of the journey before you embark" said Jesus. "You have chosen to exchange your understanding for Mine. This is a great and noble path but one in which you will encounter trouble, persecution and sometimes deep sorrow. Yet the fruit will be beyond words known by you to describe. The opening of your eyes to truth is both wondrous and terrifying. Terrifying, for the belief of man is fickle, demanding, and irrational; and you will come to know My sorrows of unbelief and doubt well.

"However, the truths I give to you to share will open many eyes and soften hardened hearts. They will be used to turn the hearts of the children to their fathers and the fathers' hearts to their children.

"The image of 'God' in the heart and mind of man is warped, incomplete, muted. I would have them to know the Father's true nature. Will you be a part of this 'heart-makeover' expedition?"

"Whatever you desire for my life, let it be without hindrance or delay," I said with a strength not my own.

"It is the Spirit of God you have received within you that gives you that strength," said Jesus. "Without the Spirit within, you can do nothing, but with Him nothing is out of your reach. Do you receive this?" He asked.

"With deep gratitude, my Lord," I affirmed.

"Very well. In order for you to see and hear deeper spiritual truths, you must learn to walk by the Spirit," Jesus said, as He wrote upon a small piece of gold paper, then folded and sealed it with His ring. He handed the paper to my angel who had been standing behind me. "You must stand upon the sure foundation before you begin this spiritual journey. Jariel will accompany and guard you."

My angel – "Jariel," as he was called by the Lord – bowed before Him.

Then Jesus took my hands in His and said, "Well done, you will not be sorry for your decision, not even in times of trouble." He stood up and pulled my face to His and said, "Remember I am always with you, always! I will never leave you nor forsake you. You are mine and I am yours. I am everything you are ever going to need."

I no longer call you servants, because a servant does not know his master's business. Instead, I have called you friends, for everything that I learned from my Father I have made known to you.   – John 15:15 (NIV)

7

MONUMENTS OF MAN

Woe to those who call evil good, and good evil;
Who substitute darkness for light and light for darkness;
Who substitute bitter for sweet and sweet for bitter!
Woe to those who are wise in their own eyes
And clever in their own sight!   – Isaiah 5:20-21

Jariel took me to a gated park. The sign above the large iron gate read "Monuments of Man."

We walked on a well-manicured path with lush pristinely-kept grass and stunning flowers (that weirdly seemed to watch us as we passed by). It was a beautiful park except for the large irregular-shaped towers of black rock scattered for miles and miles. They were all unsightly – like a lone chimney in a house destroyed by fire.

"What is this place?" I asked. "What are those odd rock structures?"

We stopped in front of a tall, very jagged rock. "Look there," Jariel said. The sign at the base bore my name. "This is your current life's monument or legacy." As I looked closer I could see the faint shape of a throne-like seat at the top of this very high stone structure. A staircase encircled the rock. The stairs were crooked, broken off in parts, all different sizes and shapes, and appeared to have been abandoned.

"I do not wish to sound irreverent, but it's quite ugly for a monument; who is making it?" I asked.

"You are!" Jariel explained. "This is the base or foundation stone of your life. It is being constructed with each and every decision you make on Earth. Each step represents an event and the choice you made," he explained. "Every trial, every disappointment, fear, triumph, every test, every temptation put before you created the riser of each step. The step itself represents your choice: to endure, to flee or escape, to blame, to attack or retreat, to have faith or doubt, to feel anger or pain. You can see that at times, the solutions to your trials were firm, strong, and wise (represented by a perfect step without flaw), yet many more times your solutions were steeped in doubt and unbelief (steps with half or no step, or jagged on one side)."

"I've made a lot of bad decisions!" I said, a bit embarrassed by the hapless, jagged appearance of my foundation stone.

"Don't worry, they are all like this; only One is perfect and flawless, only One."

"Many, when confronted with a trial that produces pain, will turn from it and run, or medicate to escape, not knowing that these trials are the stepping stones that take them above the situation to a higher level of wisdom, knowledge, and understanding. Relish these times of trial and press into your Lord. You must go through the pain in order to rise above it." Jariel took my hand and started up the staircase of my life.

"Every son and daughter of Adam has built a life monument unique to themselves," he said. As we ascended my monument, the memory of each step's event flooded over me in great detail – some pleasurable, some painful to relive. I began to notice other structures being constructed in close proximity to mine. Some of them were being built apart from the "rock platform" which seemed to be central to all the lots.

"Why do they not use the foundation stone?" I asked. "Wouldn't their tower be more secure on the stone rather than on dirt alone?"

"These are they who have rejected the cornerstone provided to them and who built their legacy upon foundations of clay, trusting in their own strength and wisdom," Jariel answered.

I watched as one ambitious man reached his summit and sat down triumphantly on his throne. "This man," Jariel said with sadness, "followed his own path, rejected God's laws and gave his life to build a name for himself in the Earth. He did not consider what awaited him after death."

The man said in his heart, "My power and the might of my hand have gotten me this wealth."

> Therefore, as a tongue of fire consumes stubble and dry grass collapses into the flame, so their root will become like rot and their blossom blow away as dust; for they have rejected the law of the LORD of hosts and despised the word of the Holy One of Israel.   – Isaiah 5:24

Jariel said, "Talent and free will accomplished much for this man, but he did not consider his end!"

A dark spirit appeared in front of the man and said, "Jesus I know, Paul I know, but who are you?"

"When confronted with the authority and power of the enemy," Jariel said, "a man on his own will be torn apart, tormented and easily destroyed." I watched as the darkness overtook the man and burned his legacy to the ground, to be remembered no more. "Such is not the will of your Father for any of His children. However, they were given free will," Jariel informed me.

> According to the grace of God which was given to me, like a wise master builder I laid a foundation, and another is building on it. But each man must be careful how he builds on it. For no man can lay a foundation other than the one which is laid, which is Jesus Christ. Now if any man builds on the foundation with gold, silver, precious stones, wood, hay, straw, each man's work will become evident; for the day will show it because it is to be revealed with fire, and the fire itself will test the quality of each man's work. If any man's work which he has built on it remains, he will receive a reward. If any man's work is burned up, he will suffer loss; but he himself will be saved, yet so as through fire.   – 1 Corinthians 3:10-15

> Therefore, as the fire devours the stubble, and the flame consumes the chaff, so their root will be as rottenness, and their blossom will ascend like dust; because they have rejected the law of the LORD of hosts, and despised the word of the Holy One of Israel.   – Isaiah 5:24 (NKJV)

Jariel continued to climb. "You can tell a lot about a human life by looking at their staircase. Some stairs become more and more perfect with age and experience. Some have long stretches of perfect steps and then hit a place that appears to have been bombed out. These structures are living testaments and lasting legacies that stand open and bare before the Lord. Make your decisions well, build them on the rock, and FOR the 'Rock.' Trust Him. He never fails."

We reached the end of the stairs; only smooth uncut rock lay above us. "We have reached your present, and your next choice."

8

PORTAL WINDOW

I looked up the steep solid rock mountain. A window was cut into the rock about twelve feet above our heads. "What is that window?" I asked Jariel.

"Ah, a rare sight on a human foundation stone, indeed!" Jariel said with excitement. "That is a 'hodos peran' portal! It is an invitation! Will you proceed through it?" he asked, eyes ablaze.

"Hodos peran portal? What does 'hodos peran' mean?" I asked. Jariel took out his dictionary, and flipped through for its meaning.

hodos – noun

    meaning: a) a way, b) a manner of thinking, feeling, deciding

peran – adverb

    meaning: beyond, on the other side

"Hodos peran!" he said gleefully. "The way to the other side!"

"The way to the other side of what? Is it safe?" I asked with hesitation.

"Will you go through it?" he asked.

I looked up at the window and was both excited and afraid.

"What's on the other side, Jariel?" I asked.

"I don't know!" he answered.

"Why don't you know? You know what it is called!" I said to him. "You live in this dimension!"

"So do you!" he retorted. "And it is on your rock!"

"Okay then, lift me up there, it is too high to reach." I said. Jariel unfurled his wings, grabbed me around the waist and flew up to the window ledge. The stone was arched at the top and framed round about in solid rock. Up close it seemed more like a cave opening than a window, but the opening was black and completely smooth and soft like velvet to the touch. I pushed on it but it held firm like solid rock. "How do I get through?" I asked.

"I don't know," he answered with a furrowed brow and intense interest. "I've only heard of these, but I have never actually seen a human engage it before." Jariel sat down and scoured the oversized dictionary which I somehow knew contained every written word in existence. I wondered how in the world he carried around such a book. Then I remembered, I was not in the world!

I set about to discover a way through the window. Perhaps there was a secret lever somewhere. If Jesus were here He would just walk right through it. I tried that but it didn't work. After exhausting every possible means I could think of, I climbed down the rock and, perplexed, sat down next to Jariel. "I've tried everything," I said. "There is simply no way through that window."

"You have been approaching the task incorrectly!" Jariel sprang to his feet. "Your mind carries the belief that you came up here in your earthly body. You cannot come here in your earthly body. No flesh can come here. This place is spirit, your flesh is still lying on your bed in your room. I looked at my body and felt my arms and hands. They seemed the same.

"You have been trying to get through that window using the knowledge and power of your flesh alone!" Jariel said, "Not by might nor by power, but by My Spirit, says the Lord!"

"So God's Spirit has to dematerialize this body for me to pass through?" I asked.

"No," he answered. "Matthew 16:19 says, 'I will give you the keys of the kingdom of heaven; and whatever you bind on Earth shall have been bound in heaven, and whatever you loose on Earth shall have been loosed in heaven!' So, by the Spirit, loose the window!"

I looked up at the window, closed my eyes and prayed, "Lord, clothe me in your Holy Spirit." The Holy Spirit appeared over me like a glowing sheet and covered me. "I give way to your most Holy Spirit, Lord," I prayed.

"Command the window to open," I heard the Holy Spirit say within me.

"Window, open!" The window instantly opened and unfolded an accordion-like staircase. The staircase, in earthly terms, would be described as being one continuous, interwoven electrical beam of light that began inside the window and grounded itself on the floor. It seemed to vibrate with power. Fascinated, I wondered how it closed, and simply said, "close." The electrical beam unwound its staircase shape and disappeared back into the window again. "Cool! Open. Close. Open. Close." I could have stayed there all day watching this staircase fold and unfold, each time picking up new data on how it worked and its infinite possibilities.

"Much more than a staircase lies above!" Jariel said with a laugh.

I started up the stairs, filled with anticipation of what lay on the other side. Emerging through the window, I was hit by a massive "river of knowledge." Stars and darkness were all around. It was as if the sky on Earth had grown a billion-fold and the knowledge of all of it hung over me with a weight I could not bear. My senses strained for relief and I retreated down the stairs to a corner of my world. Curled up in a ball, I squeezed my eyes shut and shook in fear.

Jesus appeared and knelt down to comfort me. He gently smiled and said, "What were you expecting?" I opened an eye to see His smile. I heard His laugh that always gave me such peace.

"Green grass and lakes and white birds and angels," I said. "It's so big, I feel crushed." He wrapped me in His arms until the shaking subsided.

"You are still in the mindset of your flesh. To flesh, this world is beyond comprehension. Your spirit, when assisted by My Holy Spirit, is at home here. You have been brought here to educate your spirit in the possibilities and powers it carries on the Earth and in the spiritual realm. What you saw was the second heaven. We will be going into it each time you come here, now that you have broken through the window!" I fell asleep in His arms.

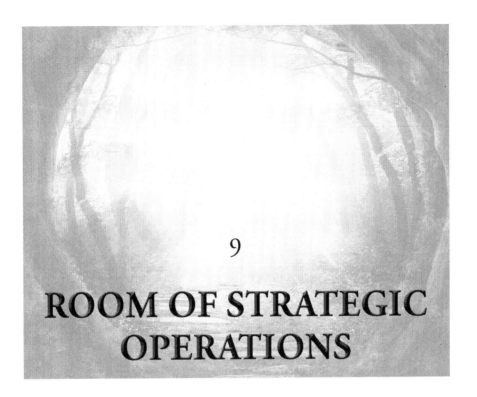

9
ROOM OF STRATEGIC OPERATIONS

When I returned, the staircase was down and a group of angels anxiously waited with Jariel. They were all packed up as if ready to leave on a backpacking trip. "Where are you all going?" I asked.

Jariel answered me, "We are going up a level. This was only a way station. The way has been opened; it is time to go up." He nodded toward the staircase. I knew I was to lead the way.

SECOND HEAVEN LEVEL

A dome-like covering made of a parachute-type material hung over the mountaintop platform. A strangely familiar angel greeted us at the entrance. As I looked closely at this angel, I noticed its appearance resembled me. Jariel introduced us, "This is one of your guardian angels."

We shook hands and I asked why angels look like those they guard. Jariel explained that angels may know more than we do about the heavenly realm but are also able to learn quite a bit about the Father by watching our lives and analyzing our decisions. "You were made in the very likeness of God Himself," my guardian angel explained. "You resemble what you focus upon. I have focused intensely on you since the time of your conception in the heart of the Lord." My face immediately blushed with the thought of having been watched all my life.

We gathered around a long white oval table that stood in the middle of the room. There was a total of twenty-six angels and myself. Within the center of the table were odd-shaped pieces spread evenly in a row. Their shapes were not of this world. The angels all closed their eyes and placed their hands upon the rim of the table. As I followed, an electrical pulse shot through my hands, up my arms and into my heart, mind and eyes. It startled me, but it was not painful. A white light within the table traveled round and round under the hands, as if probing the hearts and minds of all participants. When it stopped under a pair of hands, the color would change and that angel would speak what he was getting in prayer. When he spoke, the pieces on the table would move according to his words. This was the strategy table and each piece represented a part of the divine plan. With each input, the plan was "played out" before everyone's eyes – revealing weaknesses, strengths and outcomes to the suggested plan. Fantastic, I thought. All done in decency and order with great respect for everyone's ideas. Plans, strategies and risk factors were established here.

The light stopped under Jariel's hands. He began to pray, "I put forth the order of the Lord which has been laid upon me to accomplish. Before you today is the child of God selected for this mission. Let us begin by displaying the issue the Almighty God wants addressed. Upon this table, let the condition of the hearts of man be seen upon the Earth today."

Instantly a swirl of light began to spin in the middle of the table, emitting pieces of a 3D holographic picture which took the form of Planet Earth. It was astonishing in that it wasn't just a picture of the globe with continents and seas, it was Planet Earth full of people going about their daily routines – in real time! If I looked upon just the South American continent, I could see every single person on it. I could zero in on a single country or town or just one person and not only watch what they were doing but also know what they were thinking, feeling, and desiring. If I looked at the whole planet at once, I could see the alliances between the nations. I zeroed in on the fact that Europe, Asia, and Africa were all the same color. "Fantastic!" I cried out loud. I was so caught up in the massive vision, I didn't hear Jariel trying to ask me a question.

Jariel raised his hands from the table and the vision vanished, snapping me back to my environment. "Wow, that was the most incredible thing I have ever experienced!" I shouted with excitement. "I could see what people and nations were planning, what they wanted, when they were lying, alliances they were making, everything! I could even see the design of people's ideas placed in their hearts that they hadn't conceived of yet. Do you know what you could accomplish on Earth with all that knowledge and insight? Can we turn it back on?" I asked, beyond excited.

All of the angels' faces were stern, surprised and questioning.

"What?" I asked. "Did I say something wrong?"

Jariel spoke up as all the angels conversed quietly amongst themselves. "A human's capacity to see, know and understand is different from that of the angels. We have never had a human at the table before and therefore the concern is about what the effect this depth of knowledge and insight into your own species may have on the motives of your heart in a fallen state. For you see from a very different perspective than what we angels see."

I was perplexed. Jariel explained, "Angels come here to study God's great creation by observing man's choices, their interactions between each other, their environment, and their God. We glean insight into the heart and character of God by watching those He created in His image. We desire to understand the motives of your heart and your desire for knowledge. To understand you is to help understand our Creator."

"Let me show you what he means," my guardian angel said. "I know how visual you are, and I think this will help you understand." The angel placed his hands on the table. "Let the world of the squirrel and sparrow appear before us," he said. The globe appeared again, but this time I could only see squirrels and sparrows. "Do you know their thoughts and the intents of their hearts?" the angel asked.

"No," I said, "I can only surmise why they are doing what they are doing."

"Exactly as we see your world," the angel explained. "You can only look at the ways of this species with the comparative perspective of your own world. Many things are foreign to you in the world of the squirrel and sparrow, particularly the motivations of their hearts and why they do what they do. Thus it is for us when we look upon the inhabitants of Earth."

"Although man was created a little lower than the angels," Jariel added, "On Earth, when the age of man has ended, man will rule over and judge the angels, as men are in the image of and likeness of God Himself."

Know ye not that we shall judge angels?
– 1 Corinthians 6:3 (KJV)

"This is why Lucifer hates you so," my guardian angel warned. All this information was swelling my brain.

Jariel directed everyone back to the table. "The Lord would have your prayers be a part of this plan. However, I shall give you your limitation," he said, looking directly at me. "It has not been granted for you to observe anything more than the spiritual condition of man's heart for God at this time. You must set your mind to this task alone. All other inquiries and curiosities are forbidden to you in your fallen state. This boundary is for your own good. Do you understand?"

"Yes," I answered. I did understand well. The experience triggered that feeling of addiction, of wanting more and more. No man could stand before this vision untouched by his fallen nature, no matter how pure they were on Earth. I wondered why the Lord had shown me this.

"What stirs in the heart of man eventually appears in his world," Jariel said, with eyes closed and hands on the table. I placed my hands slowly on the table and closed my eyes. "Keep me within my limits, my Lord," I prayed.

> O that there were such an heart in them, that they would fear me, and keep all my commandments always, that it might be well with them, and with their children for ever!
> — Deuteronomy 5:29 (KJV)

> And God saw that the wickedness of man was great in the earth, and that every imagination of the thoughts of his heart was only evil continually.   — Genesis 6:5 (KJV)

10

FORCES OF LIGHT AND DARKNESS

The globe once again appeared, but this time a thick black cloud formed and began weaving itself into the white fluffy clouds. Jariel commanded, "Let the cloud covering be removed and the second heaven activity revealed!" The clouds appeared to thin out, revealing a hoard of angelic and demonic activity. I saw portals stationed strategically around the globe, each one centered above a governing place of power – Washington, D.C., Beijing, Paris, London, Berlin, Moscow, Tokyo, Rome, Ottawa, Madrid and others. Large portals and small ones bustled with both angelic and demonic activity. Each was controlled by either the forces of light or the forces of darkness. I somehow knew that control of those portals was determined by the hearts and prayers of those below its territory.

I zeroed in on the portal of America and saw a great battle raging for control of its portal. My eyes locked on the prince of the dark angel forces who fought for control of the USA portal; I listened as he commanded his army.

"Conquer this portal and burn its banner, 'One Nation Under God'! Conquer this portal and its banner shall be, 'One Nation Under My Feet'! Control this portal and prevent heaven's aid and voice from reaching mankind. Without it, man will forget about God and lean upon himself. We easily defeat a man who's on his own! If you control the portal, you control the hearts of the nation below. If you control the majority, you will pit brother against brother."

> Then he said to me, "Do not be afraid, Daniel, for from the first day that you set your heart on understanding this and on humbling yourself before your God, your words were heard, and I have come in response to your words. But the prince of the kingdom of Persia was withstanding me for twenty-one days; then behold, Michael, one of the chief princes, came to help me, for I had been left there with the kings of Persia.
> – Daniel 10:12-13

The prince then gave orders to a legion of dark angels to enter the earthly realm. "Go, win the hearts of these profane creatures, cause them to turn their backs to God and all His rules, and bow before me! Convince them it is the better way. Tell them there are no rules in my kingdom to keep them from their lusts. Tempt their weak flesh with seductions; release discord and strife in those who believe in God, for it will break the strength of their union. Tell them good is evil and evil is good, for those who believe you will set themselves against those who do not. A house divided against itself shall fall! Don't bother to return empty-handed! Succeed, and these vile creatures God loves so much will lick your boots, not rule over you!"

The horde of demons erupted in cheers and shot through the portal into the Earth below, carrying with them many schemes, devices, and ploys to seduce and deceive man into relinquishing his glorious destiny in Christ.

Finally, be strong in the Lord and in the strength of His might. Put on the full armor of God, so that you will be able to stand firm against the schemes of the devil. For our struggle is not against flesh and blood, but against the rulers, against the powers, against the world forces of this darkness, against the spiritual forces of wickedness in the heavenly places. – Ephesians 6:10-12

Jariel explained, "An angelic army's strength and number are determined by the prayers, faith, and accord of the children below. There is great power amassed in, and for, the heavenly hosts when men pray in agreement with one another. Both for good and for evil."

Again I say unto you, That if two of you shall agree on earth as touching any thing that they shall ask, it shall be done for them of my Father which is in heaven.   – Matthew 18:19 (KJV)

"Was this why God confused the language at the Tower of Babel?" I asked.

"Yes," Jariel answered. "At the time of Babel, the hearts and intents of man had begun to unite with the dark prince's ways. Darkness had gained control of every seat of influence. The book of Isaiah tells of Satan's fall."

But you said in your heart, "I will ascend to heaven; I will raise my throne above the stars of God, and I will sit on the mount of assembly, in the recesses of the north. *I will ascend above the heights of the clouds;* I will *make myself* like the Most High."
                                        – Isaiah 14:13-14

"Satan taught the sons of Adam these same evil ways of pride infusing man's pure language with perverse words and understanding," said Jariel. "This understanding led the entire race of men onto Satan's path of destruction."

They said, "Come, let us build for ourselves a city, and a tower *whose top will reach into heaven*, and let us *make for ourselves a name*, otherwise we will be scattered abroad over the face of the whole earth."   – Genesis 11:4

"God Himself had to intervene or nothing would have been impossible for the dark forces to do – with and through the children of men," Jariel said.

The LORD said, "Behold, they are one people, and they all have the *same language*. And this is what they began to do, and now nothing which they purpose to do will be impossible for them."   – Genesis 11:6

"This confusion of language forced a split in the allegiance of man to the ruler of darkness," said Jariel. "You cannot agree with someone you do not understand!"

"Yes, I see that now." I answered. "Will they conquer that portal and darken the land I love?"

"The human heart is the most deceitful of all things, and desperately wicked. Who really knows how bad it is? But I, the LORD, search all hearts and examine secret motives. I give all people their due rewards, according to what their actions deserve."
                                         – Jeremiah 17:9-10 (NLT)

"Their actions are what are rewarded. The prayer of a righteous man accomplishes much, but will the Lord find prayer and faith at the time of His return?" Jariel asked.

Now He was telling them a parable to show that at all times they ought to pray and not to lose heart, saying, "In a certain city there was a judge who did not fear God and did not respect man. There was a widow in that city, and she kept coming to him, saying, 'Give me legal protection from my opponent.' For a while he was unwilling; but afterward he said to himself, 'Even though I do not fear God nor respect man, yet because this widow bothers me, I will give her legal protection, otherwise by continually coming she will wear me out.'" And the Lord said, "Hear what the unrighteous judge said; now, will not God bring about justice for His elect who cry to Him day and night, and will He delay long over them? I tell you that He will bring about justice for them quickly. However, *when the Son of Man comes, will He find faith on the earth?"* — Luke 18:1-8

The vision of the battle in the heavens shook me for days. Lord, forgive us for our apathy and inaction. Oh, that we would all pray in unison as one.

11

THE HOUSE OF WISDOM

"In My Father's house are many dwelling places; if it were not so, I would have told you; for I go to prepare a place for you. If I go and prepare a place for you, I will come again and receive you to Myself, that where I am, there you may be also."

– John 14:2-3

What do these dwelling places look like? Who builds them? Does everyone have one? Do we live with relatives there or alone? I had been pondering John 14:2-3 and asked the Lord if I had a mansion and what it looked like.

"Do you want to see it?" He asked.

"Yes!" I exclaimed.

My spiritual eyes opened, and I found myself sitting on a boat dock, flipping my feet in the crystal-clear water of an enormous lake. I was fascinated with the water that seemed to be lit from below, like a swimming pool with its light on at night. The sound of the water was different, as well. As I pinpointed my focus on the lapping ripples, I began to hear a rhythm and tinkling of a song resonating and vibrating through my entire being. I could have sat there absorbing the water alone for hours.

"Come and see the house!" I heard the Lord say behind me. Everything felt thicker, solid, more real here. The same as Earth but different, authentic, not just a shadow but the actual original design. The colors hit the sensors in my eyes and brought great pleasure. You cannot walk fast here because the sights and sounds overtake you. "Your appreciation and wonder for My Kingdom fills My heart with delight, beloved," Jesus said. I was simply unable to speak. Jesus took my hand and led me up the dock to the house on the hill.

The path was a deep, rich soil, bordered by brilliant green grass and a happy row of beautiful tulips. I love tulips, they always make me so happy. As we mounted the steps to the house, I was struck by the solid gold memorial plate deeply engraved on the white pillar which bore my name. Jesus said, "This is your house, prepared with everything you have come to love and cherish. I have watched you your whole life and made note of each and every delight of your heart. It's all here!" He said, His wonderful eyes sparkling with love and excitement.

"My words of gratitude would not be enough, my Lord, to express my love and appreciation. Give to me the words my heart is feeling right now and I will gladly pour them over You!" I pleaded.

He took my face in His hands and placed His forehead on mine. "You will be with Me for all eternity. You haven't seen anything yet, this is only the beginning!"

It is written, "Things which eye has not seen and ear has not heard, and *which* have not entered the heart of man, all that God has prepared for those who love Him."

– 1 Corinthians 2:9

The tour of the house was deeply profound and personal as it truly contained everything I loved and cherished on Earth, both tangible things and intangible. Some I had long forgotten but He had not forgotten. Everything I had lost on Earth was there, everything I had always wanted was there. Marble countertops, beautiful wood floors and a lakefront view! I stood in awe of all the tiny details He had thought of for me, like the six-inch baseboards, roaring fireplace and stunning multicolored tulips. This is our future with Him; we will not be disappointed in what lies ahead of us; we who love Him. Oh, that you would love Him! He has done all of this for you.

"You can come here whenever you like," Jesus said. "Let this be your place of refuge and peace."

From that day on, when I am in need of comfort or quiet intimate fellowship with the Lord, I come here in the spirit and find peace and wisdom.

WISDOM'S HOUSE

Such was this day. I had come back here in spirit to clear my head from the hustle and bustle of life on Earth, and I had been drawn to the water. I plunged my head into the water to "clear it" and I found it refreshing. This particular day, as I watched the amazing fish observing me, I heard a laugh. As I emerged, I saw the Lord approaching in a boat. "Just your head, huh?" He asked with a smile. The Lord pulled the boat up to the dock and asked, "Would you like to go for a ride? There is someone special I want you to meet."

"Okay," I said and leaped into the boat. Here I was, sitting in a boat with the King of Glory, and my mind kept drifting to the cares of the world. In and out of the spirit I went.

"Stay with Me, love," I heard Jesus say. I had come to know that these distractions always came before a major revelation, so I pressed in and focused. We stopped in the middle of the lake. "We get out here," Jesus said, and stepped out onto the water. Okay! I knew I was in the spirit and could walk on the water, too. I leaped out and glided to a stop. This was so amazing. I ran fast and then slid, like on snow or ice, spraying water. Again, I could have spent hours exploring the possibilities.

"Plenty of time for that later. Come," Jesus said as He began walking up a staircase that formed with each step He took. As if by His sheer will to go up, the means materialized to accommodate Him.

"How do I make the step appear like You did?" I asked Him.

"Follow Me," He answered.

I lifted my leg as if to take a step up and as my foot came down, a stair appeared. Then another and another. We ascended through several layers of realms, like worlds stacked on top of worlds, where the ceiling of one world became the floor of another. When we reached the level we were going to, I heard the sound of an elevator bell ring but noticed the sound and light were combined somehow. The sound of the bell released a different form of light. I wondered if the light here was composed of a different kind of molecule than our lights on Earth.

We got off and were greeted by a supremely dressed company of officials. The first thing I noticed was their awe of Jesus. Their eyes sparkled with deep reverence and love for Him, which I could only equate with the awe of those meeting the President or a favorite rock star – only this awe was pure.

We went by foot up a path that ended at a huge house perched high above an enormous lake. I wondered if all the lakes lined up in all the realms, like plumbing pipes in our houses here on Earth.

This house was built of rich mahogany wood, with every detail perfected; even the water running under the foot bridge dripped onto flowers in a melodic way that bent my mind. The escort opened the door without a knock, so I presumed it was his house, but the Lord read my thoughts and said, "There is no need to knock here." I began to ask myself why we knocked on doors before entering on Earth. My answer was to give the tenants warning of your approach, to give them time to clean up if they needed to, to be polite and not just barge in unannounced. Jesus said He knocked on our hearts and waited for us to open to Him. "Doors represent choices, but here the choice is determined when the house is built," Jesus explained.

We entered the house and were greeted by a remarkable woman whose appearance was that of an Italian woman in her late sixties; she had warm brown eyes and was about five feet tall. Her eyes were kind, full of love and deep knowledge. She looked at me as if she knew more about me than I knew about myself. "Welcome to our home," she said, wrapping me in her warm arms of love. I recognized the voice immediately.

"You are her, the voice I hear all the time! You are Wisdom!" I exclaimed.

"Yes, my dear one, it is I, and I am overjoyed to meet you, spirit to spirit. We have much to catch up on!" she said to me.

THE ASSIGNMENT

Jesus looked deep into my eyes and said, "Here you will find all the answers to the many and varied questions you seek —the true meaning of life and your purpose in it. I encourage you to go as deep as you like into Wisdom's storehouse of knowledge. It will fare well with you to do so."

I felt as if I were a teenager being left at the gates of a college – excited and a bit nervous. The pass from His arms to hers was warm and safe. The lessons began immediately.

Wisdom wrapped her warm loving arms around me, "Come, I will show you to your room," she said.

The beautiful mahogany floors were spotted with rich carpets. The room was lit with the warm glow of candles in the night; it was the embodiment of cozy. The bed was adorned with rich cotton, fluffy pillows and beautiful silk, such that one would never want to leave. Everything spoke to me of rest and refreshment. The window circled the room from floor to ceiling, overlooking the vast lake below.

THE MYSTERY

Again, everything in the room was pleasant to my taste and style; everything but one item that captured my attention. It was an odd item that sat in the windowsill. Its shape had no uniform pattern to it and it appeared old and deformed. I picked it up and found it much heavier than I expected. It appeared to be a shriveled-up, petrified apple core, completely out of place here. "What is this?" I asked Wisdom.

"This is the reason you were brought here. Its meaning and purpose will take you some time to comprehend. You must take this on your journey and keep it with you always." She tied a string to it and placed it around my neck. "When comprehension comes, you will treasure this with your life!"

That night I slept in that wonderful bed, surrounded by warmth, comfort and beauty. But I could not think of anything else but the mystery of the trinket that now hung around my neck.

12

FAITH UNDER FIRE

Wisdom's favorite room in her house is her kitchen, where she is always preparing something that fills the atmosphere with a warm, inviting aroma. I sat at her kitchen table and watched her cook.

Jesus appeared, "I am going to reveal to the eyes of your spirit the beginning of all things," He said. "You will write down what you are shown as a testimony to the world of My purposes and intents for all creation. It has long been forgotten and watered down. This is the time for the restoration of all things and a restoration of My true face in the Earth. Will you go?"

I fell into His arms, "Oh, Lord, you know it is the cry of my heart to see Your Kingdom come and Your Will done in the Earth. I so long to see, out of the abundant outpouring of gratitude and love for You, that every knee bows and every tongue confesses that You are Lord!" I cried. The passion deep within me was being called forth by His embrace. "Yes, I will go!" I said as I looked up into His eyes of love. I knew multitudes would come to Him if they really knew Him.

Knowing about Him was one thing, but to know Him intimately was to love Him unconditionally.

SHIPS OF LIGHT

Jesus took my hand and led me to the balcony overlooking the lake. He pointed to the water which had seven enormous "ships of Light" anchored side by side. These ships appeared to be made of light beams. "You will be accompanied by, and come to know well, My Spirit – Wisdom, Knowledge, Counsel, Might, Fear of the Lord, and Understanding. These will prepare you to receive, to carry and to deliver the revelation to the world. Step by step, dear one, line upon line, precept upon precept. Nothing before its time. Let's pray. 'Father of all Glory, hallowed be Thy name in all creation. As You have sent Me, so I send this child. Be filled without measure, be transformed by the renewing of your mind so that you may see, know and understand the depth of Our love for you and all the children in the Earth.'"

A LIFE SO ORDERED

"Tell me how you would like to see your life ordered?" He asked me.

I thought a moment and answered, "Quiet, peaceful, orderly, full of divine encounters, supernatural healings, and the presence of God. With an orderly, patterned routine that leads to healing and growth. The wisdom of Jesus poured out in abundance for the glory of God. The law of God honored and obeyed. The Name of our Father hallowed in all the land. The fear of the Lord tangible in every decision we make. God's kingdom come, present all the time. His will done every day, every minute, every second. A home for me and my husband that is our own in the neighborhood I love. A mountain cabin for times of rest and refreshment. An internet network connecting the Body of Christ. My niece working for me, married with children. My family and friends reconciled, happy and healthy and healed. Our inheritance and finances managed by Wisdom herself. To have our ministry and network be a haven for the world to find wisdom, the law of God, peace, guidance, and salvation for billions of souls."

Jesus was handed a pen and paper by an angel standing behind Him. The angel stood tall, strong and watchful. Jesus wrote an "Order of the King" and gave it to the angel, who bowed and flew away. "So let it be ordered," He said. "Doubt not and it shall be."

"How do I combat doubt, Lord?" I asked Him. He pointed to His heart and head as if to say, "It begins in the heart and gives order to the mind. Doubt is fear manifested. It is an actual tangible substance, just like hope."

FROM FAITH TO FACT

I looked at Him and wondered how I could ever doubt even a single word that He spoke. If He said, "Let it be ordered," then it was already in the works. I would see a day when every single one of the things I stated would come to pass.

"Faith transforms hope into fact and activates expectation," He said. "Your days will then be filled with action steps to that end. The evidence of your faith will begin to appear with each step you take in bringing your desire from the heavenly realm into the earthly realm. Your expectation alerts you to pieces of your faith's foundation – walls, roof, paint and décor. These pieces would have been overlooked had your faith not produced the reality of the finished work and made it fully visible to your mind's eye. Come, I will show you."

Instantly we were on a dock, boarding one of the huge ships of Light. We stepped onto the ship and were escorted to the captain's chair. "Take a seat!" Jesus said. I took a seat in the chair that instantly adjusted to my body, placing me in the perfect position to captain the big ship's steering wheel. There was a directional meter gage on top of the wheel with a red dial that locked into the coordinates chosen.

On the meter were three words. To the far left, at about 9 o'clock, was the word DOUBT. At the 12 o'clock position was the word AIMLESS and to the far right, at 3 o'clock, was the word FAITH.

"Here is how faith works." Jesus explained, "I asked you how you would like to see your life ordered. You told me and I granted your request because all parts of it lined up with My Word and My purposes for your life. I commanded the angel to let it be so ordered. Look and see!" Jesus pointed upward and a giant square sheet appeared, suspended in the sky. The picture of my life, ordered as I had asked, appeared on the sheet. As I watched, tiny lines began crawling across the picture from the four corners, cutting out tiny pieces throughout the sheet, forming a jigsaw puzzle. The puzzle then blew apart and the pieces were catapulted in a straight line headed east.

Jesus continued, "Now, if you have faith that it has already been produced and set in motion, then you will set your sail on FAITH and lock in the coordinates." He turned the wheel until it locked into the 3 o'clock position. The ship surged right and headed east. As we navigated the water, we began to come upon pieces of the puzzle floating on the water. We scooped them up with a net. "You have made your plans," Jesus said, "but I direct your steps and determine what comes into your life at what time."

We laid the pieces we had found on a large table and began to fit them together. Lightning and thunder disrupted our peaceful tranquility. The strikes were close and shook the ship. Jesus looked intently at my reaction. "Now, when you run into a bad storm on this course – which you will – and your ship is buffeted to and fro, what will you do?" Huge waves began to buffet the ship, nearly cracking the sides. My eyes went to the large swells headed our way. It's one thing to surmise what you would do in a given situation, but entirely different when you are IN the situation. My mind flew over all the possibilities. I was afraid of deep water; we could drown, or be torn apart by a shark. It was getting worse and worse. I looked for Jesus but couldn't see Him anymore. What was I to do? I was the captain. "I must make a decision," I realized.

We could go back and wait out the storm, or we could take a different course. We had to get out of the storm! I turned the ship out of the storm and locked into the 9 o'clock course. The ship slowly began to stabilize and hit on smooth water. We were headed in the opposite direction. Puzzle pieces began to appear again. "I must have made the right move!" I thought. The pieces looked just like the others, so I assumed they were part of the puzzle. I scooped them up and, as the water stilled, I once again began trying to put the pieces together.

Jesus appeared beside me and said, "So you revisited your faith and changed your mind?"

"Lord! The ship was cracking; all was about to be lost! I had to do something!" I pulled a puzzle piece out of the water and showed Him, "See, we found our way back on track!" I said.

Jesus looked stern, "Did you?"

I was perplexed.

"Look and see," Jesus said, pointing up. Another sheet appeared above us. On it was the exact opposite of what was on the first one. I didn't like that order for my life, it was full of disappointment, frustration, failure, depression, loss and death. It, too, was cut into puzzle pieces, only thrown in the opposite direction. Jesus reached into the water and pulled one of its pieces out and picked up a piece from the first puzzle, holding both up for me to see. They looked identical, however, one of them ignited in His hand and burned to ashes.

KNOW YOUR ENEMY

Jesus began, "Now, if you are tossed to and fro between two decisions, your world will be full of mixture and confusion, just as your enemy proposes. I would have you either hot or cold. But if you are full of mixture, lukewarm, I will spit you from My mouth. See and know your enemy and his ways. I would not have you ignorant of his devices, which are many!" Jesus placed his fingers on my eyes and said, "Be opened."

My eyes opened and landed on the table. The puzzle pieces had turned black and white making it crystal clear which ones were impostors. I began to pluck out the black ones and wondered why Jesus didn't allow us to always see this clearly all the time. Then I looked up from the table and saw what stood around it.

Crowded around me were the most insidious, grotesque, foul creatures I had ever seen. Their eyes burned with charismatic hatred and lust. They smiled and looked down at my hands, which were full of their dark puzzle pieces. I looked down as well and saw that their blackness had begun to seep into my skin and crawl up my arms like spilt black ink. I instinctively knew that each one of these puzzle pieces belonged to and empowered each of the creatures.

"Jesus!" I yelled, throwing the pieces at the creatures. The black stains remained on my hands, as did the creatures before me. "Go away!" I screamed at them, frantically wiping my hands on my clothing as the blackness crawled higher and higher up my arms.

"You're going to drown!" one filthy creature said with delight.

"You'll never make the journey!" another said, mockingly.

"You are afraid of the water and fell for the very first device!"

"Easy prey."

"Stupid and unworthy."

"Gullible."

"A failure, this one."

Their words hit the core of my being, addressing every single insecurity and fear that had plagued me all my life. I wanted to punch them, but the accuracy of their words disarmed the fight within me. I slumped to the floor, helplessly watching the blackness cover my arms. "Jesus, what have I done?"

With brandished sword posed to strike, my angels surrounded me. "Rise up and fight your enemy!" I heard Jariel shout.

The demons began to wax stronger, landing crushing blows on my valiant angels. "They are strong and you have given them the right to be aboard. Reverse your allegiance!" Jariel shouted.

I didn't understand and just lay there like a deer caught in headlights. "You carry more power in your tongue than we do in our swords! Resist! Resist!" A pack of demons pounced on Jariel, driving his head into the floor.

"Stop it!" I shouted. The demons gave pause as if waiting for something to land. Nothing did. The slaughter ensued.

"Use your authority! Command them!" I felt helpless and confused. One by one the angels shouted input.

"You are an heir, are you not?"

"A child of the King?"

"Act like one!"

The eyes of my understanding began to open. If I was a child of God who had been given all authority by Jesus' death and resurrection, then I carried the same power He did. He had already defeated these demons and made a mockery of their leader. "In

69

the name of Jesus..." before I could even finish my sentence the demons were repelled to the other side of the ship. They paused, as if waiting for the bomb to hit. "... I command you to leave this ship," I continued. At that, 90% of the pack disappeared. "Get out of here!" I shouted.

"No," these remaining ones replied.

Jariel came to my side, "They have a right to be here," he said. "You came into agreement with them when you changed the course of the ship. You must break your allegiance to your fears." I understood and knew that mere words would not drive these demons away, I had to demonstrate a belief in my words. He will protect me, I told myself, as I plucked up my courage, set my eyes upon my enemy, and charged them. "I said get off this ship!" As I grabbed hold of the demon to throw him overboard, he vanished.

The mysterious necklace around my neck began to glow and burned hot. I grabbed hold of it and saw a small piece of it glowing bright blue. As it "cooled," the edges under the colored area reshaped and became smooth, sparkling like a jewel. Strange, I thought.

HOT – LUKEWARM – COLD

"There will be other obstacles ahead," Jesus said, once again appearing. "Will you turn back again? Will you be like the waves of the sea tossed to and fro between faith and doubt, never reaching your destination?" Jesus asked, as He turned the ship's steering wheel into the 12 o'clock position under the word AIMLESS.

"Many set their course here between the two extremes, never plunging fully into either," He went on. "These people are useless to Me, I would rather they were hot or cold, but the lukewarm I spit from mouth.

"You overcame only when you locked fully into the faith position and depended not on your own understanding or power but on Mine. Lock into faith and break off the level so the ship cannot change its course no matter what you run into. I will be with you through all the storms and trials and will use every one of them to your benefit. This is faith."

ACKNOWLEDGE HIM

Jesus continued... "I say to you, 'In everything you do, acknowledge Me and I will crown your efforts with success.' You have not because you ask not, you ask and don't receive because you ask amiss. Be not as the waves of the sea, tossed to and fro between what you believe, for that man will receive nothing."

I stood at the bow of ship with the Lord as the ship navigated through rough waters. I was getting used to the buffeting waves. "Lord," I asked, "Many will stand here in their journey of faith and wonder, 'Have I made the right decision?' 'Am I headed in the right direction?' 'What if this isn't the path the Lord has set for me?' 'How can we be sure this direction is the right one?'"

Jesus looked at me with the look of a father amused at his little child's silly question. "Your questions suppose that I am unable to correct your path. If your toddler set a course for herself that led to a cliff, what would you do?" Jesus asked.

"My alarm would sound and I would pick her up and turn her around in the opposite direction."

"Precisely! If she were two, she would not be inclined to listen to reason but would set her desire upon that cliff. I have seen many of My angels pick up My children, kicking and screaming as a two-year-old child, and set them on the proper course. Some children have to be taken out of the park before they see the reason. I have My ways, child." He smiled. "If a child asks for an egg, will you give him a snake? Or rather, if he asks at all, will your heart not be inclined to reward him for seeking the path of wisdom instead of self-rule? When a child asks Me, 'Am I doing it right?' or 'Are you happy with this?' that concern warms my heart deeply. You can be sure that child will not only get what he asks for but be piled high with additional blessings. This is what is meant by 'Come to Me as a child.'"

13

SPIRIT OF MIGHT

I plopped down at Wisdom's kitchen table, exhausted.

"You put too much trust in those feelings of yours," Wisdom said to me. "Living by feelings is dangerous, precious one. I have someone the Lord would have you to know."

As if on cue, one with the appearance of a giant ancient Roman gladiator entered through the front door. He looked at me, sized me up, then looked down at himself, examining his clothes as if for the first time. He and Wisdom exchanged a look and laughed. "This is your impression of me?" his voice boomed.

I was confused.

Wisdom intervened, "This is the Spirit of Might, dear," she said. "He is amused at your impression and expectation of him."

"Many have me dressed this way; don't fret," Might said. "It is what you have come to know of the ancient and spiritual world." He pounded his chest and said, "So be it, then!"

Wisdom smiled broadly. "You have only your experience on Earth to form your understanding of things here. We have a bit of fun with each other now and then."

I wondered what she really looked like.

"Let's talk about what happened on that ship," Might said to me. He opened the Bible to Zechariah 4:6 and read, "'Not by might (armies) nor by power (strength of man), but by My Spirit,' says the LORD of hosts." "That would be me," Might said to me. He touched my head and said, "Let the eyes of understanding open."

My eyes landed on Might's deep, penetrating, beautiful blue eyes, so clear, so peaceful, overflowing with intelligence and power, power, power. I was lost in his eyes.

"Now that's better, is it not?" he said, observing his changed appearance. He was no longer dressed in Roman garb but a beautiful white and gold tunic, and he radiated light that formed a perfect circle rainbow around his head. I wondered if this was the rainbow that encircled the throne?

> And I saw another *mighty* angel come down from heaven, clothed with a cloud: and a rainbow was upon his head, and his face was as it were the sun, and his feet as pillars of fire.
>
> – Revelation 10:1 (KJV)

FAITH VS. EMOTIONAL CHOICES

The Spirit of Might looked into my eyes and gently asked, "What do you think drove those demons away?"

I didn't have an answer. "I'm not sure."

"Do you think it was your mighty strength that made them flee?"

"Well, when I told them to leave, it was as if they paused a moment to see if something would happen, as if waiting for a bomb to drop. When nothing happened, they remained," I surmised.

"So your command held no authority?" he asked.

"No, it didn't; they only fled when I charged them," I said.

"When you charged them, what was it you intended to do to them had they not fled?" he asked.

"To be honest, I don't know. It felt similar to chasing off pelicans at the beach – I just wanted to scare them off. Had they held their ground, I would have been in trouble," I said.

"So you fooled them into thinking you were stronger and more powerful than they were?" he asked.

"I guess," I answered, unsure.

"Are you?" he asked. "Are you stronger than the demons? Demons who have single-handedly brought down entire armies of men? Are you so wise to have fooled eternal beings whose life span compared to your own is far beyond understanding?"

I felt small and foolish. I looked to Wisdom for help.

"He has a critical lesson for you, dear. Stay with him," Wisdom said sternly.

Might picked up Wisdom's Bible, "Your Lord and mine has given you the answer here:

"Proverbs 3:5-6 states, 'Trust in the Lord with all your heart and do not lean on your own understanding. In all your ways acknowledge Him, and He will make your paths straight.'

"Philippians 2:13 (NKJV) states, 'For it is God who works in you both to will [counseling you as to what His will is] and to do [giving you His power and ability to perform that will] for His good pleasure.'

"John 15:5 (NLT): 'Without Me you can do nothing.'

"Philippians 4:13 (NKJV): 'I can do all things [only] through Christ who strengthens me.' It's not what we can do for God, but what God will do through us.

"Jeremiah 9:23-24 (NKJV) declares, 'Thus says the Lord: "Let not the wise man glory in his wisdom, let not the mighty man glory in his might, nor let the rich man glory in his riches; but let him who glories glory in this, that he understands and knows Me, that I am the Lord, exercising lovingkindness, judgment, and righteousness in the Earth. For in these I delight," says the Lord.'"

Might continued, "Fear, anger, lust, and hate are the fuel of emotional choices which quench the flow of God's Spirit. Faith choices (choices to follow Him regardless of how you feel) unleash all of His power to come to your aid. Thus, your willpower – what you choose moment by moment – is the key to whose life will emanate in your soul.

"God's Spirit of Strength in the Greek means: 'power to rein in, mastery over self, self-control or, better yet, Spirit-control.' This is exactly what God's Spirit of Strength does – it reins in (or brings into captivity) your self-life so that God's Life can come forth.

"Luke 21:19 (KJV) says, 'In your patience possess [or rein in] your souls.'

"When you make faith choices not to go by what you feel, think or want, but to go God's way, God will then give you His supernatural Strength to set aside your wild feelings, uncontrolled thoughts and self-centered desires so that you can act out of His Spirit and His Life," Might concluded.

"Now I ask you again, are you stronger than those demons?" Might asked.

"I can do all things through Christ who strengthens me!" I answered.

"Activate your faith with your words and eventually the wavering feelings within will fade," Might admonished.

But when He, the Spirit of truth, comes, He will guide you into all the truth; for He will not speak on His own initiative, but whatever He hears, He will speak; and He will disclose to you what is to come.   – John 16:13

14

ELIJAH AND THE WHITE HORSE

I opened my eyes and instantly found myself climbing a very steep rocky mountain. In front of me was an old man dressed in layers of ancient Israelite clothing with tassels on his robe, sandals on his feet, and gripping a very tall staff. I was fascinated with his robe as I examined the fine details and intricate weaving. It wasn't so much that it was particularly beautiful—it's that my spiritual vision of it was incredibly clear. He was old, but also wise and strong and well-built.

We were fighting wind and possible rainfall. Glancing behind me, I saw Jariel and my angelic escort, all with furrowed brows, their countenance focused and determined. I asked where we were going.

"Wisdom herself awaits us," was all I heard from the angel leading the pack. On the top of the peak stood Wisdom dressed in her outdoor gear. Her smile embraced the entire crew as we arrived at the place of rest she had prepared. A fire warmed us, and hot coffee was given to all as they took seats at the fire.

"What is this place?" I asked Wisdom. She pointed across the lake behind us and I could see we were on the top of the mountain opposite the lake from her house. I wondered how she had gotten here, and if she, too, had a staff. The old man who had led the way sat at the fire drinking his coffee. I looked at his face for the first time, trying to catch his eyes.

He had a well-tailored white beard and bushy eyebrows. I was a bit intimidated by him. "He is not mad, as you are thinking," Wisdom gently said to me, "only deeply concerned. Come, I will introduce you to him." I followed her, feeling a bit nervous, wondering who he was and why we were there, and what he was so concerned about. "My dear, this is Elijah. I believe you met him on your last journey with the Lord?"

The memory bloomed in my mind. Jesus had first taken me to a park in heaven for a stroll a few years back. We had encountered Elijah sitting next to a small lake. His staff lay on the green grass next to him, along with his mantle, which had been rolled up. I looked at the staff and remembered all the things he had done with it in the biblical stories.

He looked at me and said, "Your memory is of Moses, not me."

"Excuse me, sir?" I asked, perplexed.

"You think I parted the water with my staff – I parted it with the mantle. Go ahead, try it, I know that desire well when I see it." Elijah said, tossing me the staff.

Not knowing how, I just took a wild guess and thrust the tip of the staff into the water and said, "Part!" Nothing happened.

Elijah laughed and asked, "Why is it that you look to the staff to part the water? It's not a magic wand like earthly stories tell to lead you astray. The staff represents the Power and Authority. You don't need that staff to part these waters! Moses didn't part the waters with his staff, he did it with the Power and Authority that had been given to him. The lifting of the staff was simply to ensure that the people knew he was in charge and responsible for the miracles. Neither Moses nor his rod could be an effective instrument in a work which could be accomplished only by the omnipotence of God. But it was necessary that Moses appear to participate, in order that he might have credit in the sight of the Israelites, and that they would see that God had chosen him to be the instrument of their deliverance."

THE TONGUE OF MAN

"In the same way, Elisha and I parted the waters with our mantles, also symbols of Power and Authority. But you? You have been given Power and Authority from the Son of God directly, to exercise through your tongue!" he said.

I was beginning to get it, but apparently not as swiftly as Elijah thought I should. "You have all become blockheads, dull of senses, flabby, out-of-shape! Spiritual giants more concerned with your stomach than your Life-Source. Wake up, child of the Living God!" My eyes widened and my mouth dropped open.

I thought Wisdom told me Elijah wasn't angry, just ... passionate? I became afraid of making a mistake. Elijah grabbed his Bible, flipped through it and read, "And the LORD said to Moses, 'Why do you cry to Me? Tell the children of Israel to go forward. But lift up your rod, and stretch out your hand over the sea and divide it'" (Exodus 14:15-16). He looked back at me, his eyes fierce with faith. "God didn't say, 'Stretch out your hand over the sea and I will divide it.' He said for you to do it! Respect and honor that which has been given to you. Exercise it! Use it!" he demanded.

I popped back into the present moment. Elijah looked up at me from where he was sitting. "Have you been using your power and authority?"

ON EARTH AS IT IS IN HEAVEN

Deep in thought, I sat down next to him and the angels, around the crackling fire. The fire was as it is on Earth, but had no smoke. Something to do with the difference in the atmosphere, I wondered? Elijah spoke, "All that exists on Earth exists here in purity." His voice was much calmer than it had sounded earlier. "Many untapped resources exist for you on Earth. Many! They go unutilized, and multitudes perish because men's spirits have become dull and are ruled by their foolish flesh. Baseline. Elementary. No one seeks the meaning of the Almighty's words, 'My people are destroyed for lack of knowledge.' Lack of what knowledge?" he waited for me to respond.

"I do not know, sir." I answered.

"Knowledge of the presence of the Kingdom of God all around you! It is not some far-off place that requires a rocket ship to reach! It is there, on Earth now. 'The Kingdom of God has come *upon* you. (Luke 10:9)' Did He not pray, 'Let Your kingdom come. Let Your will be done on Earth as it is done in heaven'?" he asked. "Jariel!" Elijah shouted, "Look up the word *upon*."

Jariel took out his ever-present dictionary and read: "*On |än, ôn|* ... *a preposition* ... physically in contact with and supported by (a surface) ... located somewhere in the general surface area of (a place) ... as a result of accidental physical contact with ... supported by (a part of the body) ... so as to be supported or held by ... in the possession of (the person referred to) ... forming a distinctive or marked part of (the surface of)."

Elijah continued, "It is why all creation groans for the manifestation of the sons of God. All creation is waiting for its restoration from the fall, from the deep oppression that has taken root due to your choices and lack of diligence. Creation longs for the Kingdom to manifest! All that you are shown here is possible on Earth. Listen well, and diligently exercise your faith on Earth."

My mind drifted to all the possibilities this advice presented. Wisdom greater than Solomon is here, right now. Power to part waters, raise the dead, call down fire from heaven. It's all here for us right now. It's what Jesus meant when he said, "Greater miracles than these shall you do because I go to the Father." Jesus unlocked the prison doors and removed the constraints and all that hinders man's spirit. He resurrected our spirits within us that were dead to the spiritual world. But we must exercise our will and choose to give our spirits back to first place within us and lay our body and soul at the feet of Father, that His will would be done, not our own.

Once again, my necklace began to burn, and a purple light flashed upon it. I grabbed hold of the string and lifted it to my face. A small piece of the necklace had turned a brilliant purple. I caught Wisdom's eye, and she looked pleased. "A bit of revelation has taken root in your heart. This is a good thing!" she said.

Then the thought arose in me: What if this is all a deception? What if it's witchcraft or sorcery? I became cautious and backed away.

"Why do you fear?" Elijah's voice boomed, shaking me out of my doubt. "Did not Moses go head-to-head with the sorcerers and overtake them in power? Did I not call down fire from heaven, which consumed the offering and the altar and lapped up every ounce of the water? The enemy of your soul has a loud voice within you! Why do you allow it? He's a liar! A helpless pauper against a child of God. God won't let you fall, He loves you too much. Put away those foolish thoughts and be bold. Test those blasted spirits as He commanded. Child of the living God, silence those pitiful lies."

THE WHITE HORSE

A chariot led by a beautiful white horse arrived at our camp. It was a welcome sight to all of us. What drew my attention was the horse's eyes. As if human, they were filled with intelligence and ability, wonder and curiosity. Was my silent conversation with this white horse real or just in my mind's eye?

"Both," I heard Wisdom say from behind me. "You are conversing with the animal, and it is in your mind's eye! It's what you refer to on Earth as 'knowing,' but you're much more attuned here. In heaven you speak, listen, and converse with your mind, not always your mouth," she explained. "Travel is the same way. You think of a place, and you are there."

"Well, how exactly do you move from one place to the other?" I asked.

Wisdom said simply, "You pop."

"Pop?" I asked with elated wonder.

"Yes, you pop in and you pop out," she answered.

"Are they actual places or created right here where I am standing?" I asked.

"They are actual places. My house is across the lake. You forgot your coat there. To retrieve it, you simply locate the coat inside my house and pop out of here. Want to try it?"

Excited, I took her stretched out hand and in the blink of an eye, we popped out of camp into Wisdom's kitchen. My jacket lay upon her beautiful "fireplace" chair. It took my mind a moment to adjust.

"You are not used to this form of travel yet," Wisdom said. "It will take a while but with a bit of practice you'll soon become a master heavenly traveler," Wisdom said.

She continued, "Your mind, my dear, always questions, always seeks understanding. That is why you will find many of your heavenly Father's hidden things.

"Your mind is much more powerful than you realize. All things begin in the heart but it is the mind that ignites intentions and desires. The mind listens to the heart and when there is agreement, moves to make it happen. Take this coat, for example. Your heart 'wished' you had your coat to warm your body. Your mind came into agreement and began to look for a solution. Once it landed on a viable means to recover the coat, it signaled the body to move or to 'pop.' The material of spirit is much different than the material of flesh, much lighter and able to clothe itself completely."

At that she completely disappeared from my sight. I looked around and couldn't see her anywhere. She popped back in at the front door. "It is considered rude to pop in and out when you have company. Better to walk the distance and remain in fellowship!" she said with a smile. "While on Earth, thousands of spiritual beings surround you all the time but they are forbidden to pop in on man unless given permission by the Father. Those who are given the authority to pop in are only allowed to remain for a set amount of time. If they remain after that time, they lose their spiritual estate and are never permitted to return. Loathsome are they who did this in the past."

And the angels which kept not their first estate, but left their own habitation, he hath reserved in everlasting chains under darkness unto the judgment of the great day.   – Jude 1:6 (KJV)

"How do they make themselves invisible?" I asked.

"I will use the Lord's hummingbird to illustrate. When you observe a hummingbird, do its wings not beat so quickly as to become imperceptible to your human eye?" Wisdom asked.

"Oh yes, as do wheel rims on a car when they spin," I added.

"Well, angels and those of the spiritual realm operate at the speed of light and at a much higher frequency than you do on Earth," she explained.

"So all they have to do is slow down for us to see them?" I asked.

"Angels must be granted permission to make themselves visible in the Earth," Wisdom said firmly.

15

THRONE OF
THE HEART

"And this brings me to your lesson for the day about communication..." We had just finished our discussion about angels and, without taking a breath, Wisdom continued.

"The Lord desires for you to have further understanding of the inner workings of divine and earthly communication. This understanding will assist you in laying a proper foundation for your life work. For the motive of the heart is the foundation stone of any endeavor."

"I'm hungry, are you?" Wisdom asked. I nodded. She took my hand, "Come and see what the Lord has sent for us to eat!"

At that, my mind went back to the eyes of the horse that had arrived with the chariot wagon. We popped out of the kitchen and popped back at the campsite. My eyes locked onto the beautiful eyes of the white horse, that acknowledged my return with a twinkling smile, not with his mouth but with his eyes.

I followed Wisdom around the fire to the wagon and stopped to greet the horse. It is strange petting an animal with so much intelligence and reason. "My earthbound brothers are no different," I sensed him say. My mind went to my niece who has the gift of speaking with and understanding animals on Earth. "She sees, she knows," the horse added.

I hugged his head and thanked him for the insight. "I feel such a bond with you."

"Come and feast," I heard Wisdom say. The wagon was endless; I could not see its end. It was adorned with a beautiful, ornate, marble canopy with the words "Daily Bread" carved into its arch. I wondered "how in the world" did my horse friend pull this thing? The angels and men, women, and children in the camp took plates and began to pick and choose whatever called to them. It was not like a buffet on Earth where you stand in line and pass by each dish one at a time. Everyone went up at once, shuffling back and forth amongst one another in perfect harmony, like a well-choreographed dance. I found I just knew where everything was that I wanted, and when I arrived at its location on the wagon, the path was clear—no waiting! The color of each item danced with the scent of another and, as it was placed on a plate, it changed its shape to fit perfectly with the other selections. "Wow," I thought, "my senses have become so dull on Earth."

When my plate was full, I made my way to the long table that had been set on the opposite side of the wagon. Everyone took a seat there. I noticed the pattern that had formed by the display of different food choices, arrayed on all the plates across the table. The colors of the food formed an amazing picture of a peaceful meadow sprinkled with brilliant flowers bordering a glistening lake. A picture of perfect peace and harmony. There had been no seat assignments—how could this have happened by chance?

"There is no such thing as 'chance' here or on Earth," Elijah boomed. "Chance is a theory formed by man to explain away that part of his nature that he no longer understands, that he cannot explain with knowledge acquired solely from the soul and flesh," he added, pulling me back down into my seat. Captured by the beauty of the picture, I had unknowingly "popped out" about fifty feet above the table to get a better look, and then had popped back in.

Elijah sat to my far right at the end of the table. The seat at the head was empty, and I could not see the other end because the table was so long. This was not a picnic table nor a portable table. It was made of solid marble and was draped in the finest linen, set with solid gold utensils and plates of crystal.

Wisdom explained, "The choices made in the food line were dictated by the hunger, needs, and desires of the individual as a whole—body, soul and spirit. Each one around this table is in complete harmony with the will of Father, as well as with all parts of themselves—body, soul, and spirit. Hence the beautiful pattern that you noticed."

Elijah added, looking at me, "Everyone, that is, except for you. You still have a ways to go." I looked down at my plate and saw that its contribution to the picture had broken the lines, as if something had dropped onto a painting, distorting its form. I was horrified and embarrassed. Elijah chuckled, "Don't fret. No one here took their first seat at this table any differently than you did."

I looked up at the people and angels seated at the table and wondered, "Are the people around this table like me, just visiting?"

Elijah answered, "Yes, they have been here longer and have come into their place of harmony. You will reach that harmony if you continue to come here and eat your daily bread, the food of knowledge that He has prepared just for you." I wondered if I would meet some of these people on Earth and be able to converse about our experiences here.

THE SPIRIT OF KNOWLEDGE

The "driver" of the wagon stepped up to the table and said, "Shall we pray?" I instinctively knew he was the Spirit of Knowledge. He wore an enormous baker's hat and apron with a large leather belt and a sword hung on the belt. I bowed my head and shut my eyes in prayer. "Father of All," Knowledge prayed, "We give thanks for this, our Daily Bread, provided by your loving hand for our sustenance, refreshment, equipping, enlightenment and pleasure. You are all we need, all we desire, all we praise. Come now and sup with us."

When I opened my eyes, the light was so bright I couldn't see anything in front of me. "Welcome to the table. I'm glad you made your way here." I knew that voice and turned to see Him but was blinded by the light which sparkled with all kinds of brilliant colors.

"Lord, I can't see!" I exclaimed.

"Use the eyes of your spirit, My love, not your soul."

THE HEART THRONE

I squeezed my eyes shut and saw my soul sitting on the throne of my heart. "This is not your place!" my spirit said, with a firmness that surprised me. "As for me and my house, we shall with humility and honor serve the Lord. Pride of man, get off that throne and get behind me!"

THE EYES OF GRACE

When I opened my eyes I could now see. My plate was empty. I looked at the Lord. When He is near, there is nothing else of interest. My eyes met His, and everything in me just melted. The love that emanates from those eyes is like nothing found on Earth. Those eyes emit the substance of love, and it fills your being like warm honey, electrifying every nerve ending. His smile draws out and embraces your smile, spinning you around in a delirious dance. I learned long ago not to question whether or not I deserved, or was worthy of, that smile or that love. I knew I had done nothing to deserve that most precious gift. It was undeserved, unmerited favor from the Creator of the world, and it gave Him great pleasure that I received, opened, and cherished that amazing gift of love. This is what He endured the cross for, the joy that was set before Him, the ability to trade smiles of love with us.

ADAM AND EVE'S CHOICE

The Spirit of Knowledge whispered in my ear, "You see what He has done for mankind? He has restored you to Himself by removing that fatal choice made by Adam and Eve to experience self-rule. For the knowledge of good and evil presented them with a choice to make as to which path to follow—God's way (simple obedience to the commands of God) or the evil one's temptations. Since the knowledge, once given, cannot be taken back, man had to be empowered with His power to live according to the Father's commands, for the ways and sins had become too pervasive and persuasive. See His hands?"

I looked down at the Lord's hands and wrists, which bore the scars of the nails that had pierced through them. Tears welled up in my eyes at the horror of something so evil being done to someone so pure. The Spirit of Knowledge said, "Ah, you see the love for Him that resides in your heart? That love, combined with His power, cannot be touched or even approached by the forces of evil. It is a lethal combination and the strongest force known in all eternity. He is all you will ever need!"

"Go again and fill your plate, now that your spiritual eyes are in use," Jesus said. I got up from the table and was instinctively drawn to certain selections and portions. Filling my plate was like painting a picture. I returned to the table and placed my plate back down in its place. The addition to the whole fit much better but was still a bit off in places. "That will do just fine for now," Jesus smiled. "You will always be able to see if you are flowing in the Father's will by how your plate contributes to the whole." I looked at His plate and studied His choices, trying to figure out how to be more like Him.

16

ON EARTH AS IT IS IN HEAVEN

"Welcome to the table, My beloved," Jesus said, addressing the entire assembled group. "Let us give glory to the Father." They all in unison began to pray. I could not tell if the interpretation of the words was actually being spoken aloud or if they just began filling my internal storehouse of knowledge.

This is what I heard:

"**Our** (Jesus's and ours) **Father** (the word Abba is an Aramaic word that would most closely be translated as "Daddy." It was a common term that young children would use to address their fathers. It signifies the close, intimate relationship of a father to his child, as well as the childlike trust that a young child puts in his "daddy."), **who art in heaven** (there are two distinct places, heaven and Earth, there and here, yet one is upon the other, not adjacent to it), **hallowed** (respected, revered, feared, honored, obeyed, adopted as our own, loved) **be Thy Name** (a name that when spoken out loud releases power and carries great authority. His Name thus honored and held in the highest position of esteem by the majority releases astonishing power and blessing to believers).

"**Thy Kingdom** (God's order of laws, regulations, manipulation of elements, order of authority, power and provisions, resources, miracles, mercy, love, intolerance, justice, wrath and ways) **come,** (break forth and be established as the norm in this realm right now, reordering all that is out of alignment and empowering us for the supernatural), **Thy Will** (God's plans and purposes, intention and assertion, reason and goal, not ours) **be done** (performed, accomplished and established now and in the future, come into alignment and agreement) **on Earth** (in this current realm which man has regulated to a purely physical realm, let the Spirit of God activate the reality of the spiritual realm) **as it is in** (indicating another place or another way in which the miraculous is possible all the time. In a sense, let this earthly realm be just like it is in heaven above) **heaven** (the place where God lives and where we were made to live now, not merely in the future after we die).

"**Give us** (provide to us from this realm of heaven) **this day,** (meaning we need to come here every single day to make this request) **our daily bread** (spiritual and physical needs, wisdom, knowledge, understanding, provision, power, might, marching orders, inspiration, blueprints, corrections, lessons, etc.) **and forgive us our sins/ debts** (each day help us understand how and why we made wrong choices, sins of commission or omissions that we may come to know, understand and turn from), **as we forgive those who sin against us** (use the exact same manner and measure in which we forgive our brothers and sisters here on Earth to forgive us our sins. Wow, the measure you use to forgive others will be used by God on you. Best to make sure that measure is large and generous!)

"**Lead us** (indicating that God will lead us if we ask in the Way in which we should go this day) **lest we fall into temptation** (if we

94

do not seek His leading every day, we will be led astray down a path that seems right to us but that ends in death: death of callings, assignments, gifts, births of children).

"**For thine is the Kingdom,** (the Kingdom belongs to and is under His authority and rule and we agree to submit to that rule, not seek it for ourselves to rule and reign over) **the Power** (this power that man so desperately seeks for himself belongs to God alone. The quest for this power rules and fuels man's desire for self-regulation. The reality of man wielding this Power of God is ridiculous when viewed with eyes wide open), **and the Glory** (the glory is also what man seeks to bathe in and take the credit for himself. This, too, is pure vanity and the man who seeks it for himself will be taken down and publicly humiliated just as satan was by the Lord), **forever and ever** (into all eternity and never, ever be transferred or taken over by another, ever). **Amen** (Your amen is like a voice-activated signature on a contract, meaning: 'I am in full agreement with these terms of covenant')."

Wow, I had never experienced the fullness of that prayer before! Jesus had given us the entire purpose of His life, death, and resurrection in one short prayer, packed full of truth and love.

SPIRITUAL BODY BUILDING

Everyone began to eat their meals. As I ate, I could instantly feel the food begin to nourish and refresh my body, soul, and spirit, particularly with lots of activity around my heart and the top of my head—like the feeling of peppermint oil. I could feel my eyes expand, like a balloon being blown back up to its fullness. Every bite brought a new sensation to another part of my body. The sense that poured over me was of a building being erected, one small step at a time, becoming higher and stronger with each bolt and brick. The taste of the food electrified my senses and fascinated my mind. The conversations around me began to blend together, and I became completely absorbed in the meal and its effects on my body. I could actually feel my arm and leg muscles building up and getting stronger with every bite, as well as things being dissolved and removed.

As I followed the last rolling pea on my plate with my fork of gold, I heard the Lord address me directly, "I have much to show you, beloved one. Will you come here and sup with Me every day?"

The enormity of the invitation overwhelmed me. I found I could not look at Him. I knew my weaknesses and my easily distracted mind. What if I said, "Yes, I will," and then forgot to come, or set it aside for a later time? The words feebly dribbled out of my mouth, "I am weak and undisciplined. I will forsake the invitation. I just know I will."

"Your flesh is indeed weak, but each meal you partake of with Me here will strengthen your spirit to take its rightful rule within you. Right now it is weak, unexercised, undisciplined. That will change, I promise you."

Suddenly I realized that I was sitting alone at this table with the Lord. I so wanted to look at Him but I couldn't lift my eyes. Shame and unworthiness hung on me like a thick wet blanket. "Remember, you are 'in' Me," Jesus said firmly. That voice – I'll call it the "definition voice" – rang out in my head again.

There is therefore now no condemnation to those who are in Christ Jesus, who do not walk according to the flesh, but according to the Spirit. For the law of the Spirit of life in Christ Jesus has made me free from the law of sin and death. For what the law could not do in that it was weak through the flesh, God did by sending His own Son in the likeness of sinful flesh, on account of sin: He condemned sin in the flesh, that the righteous requirement of the law might be fulfilled in us who do not walk according to the flesh but according to the Spirit. – Romans 8:1-4 (NKJV)

I looked up at Him.

"Got it?" Jesus asked me.

"Yes Lord, I understand," I said.

"There is a time to patiently wait upon Me, but you must wait in an active state of anticipation, not a passive state. Stir up the gifts within you by actively seeking them out. I will put My Spirit of Wisdom into all who seek after it, to help them to will and to do My good pleasure."

17
THE BOOK OF LIFE

The room was thick with reverent expectation and the presence of God's power. Sitting upon a large throne was a man with the title, "Recorder." He was dressed all in white with a long flowing beard that shouted "ancient and wise." The biggest book I have ever seen sat open in front of him. Angels stood in line to present their peculiar scrolls to the man who would record their contents into the great book. Once he transcribed the scroll's contents, he would write something on a piece of paper and hand it to the angel. The angel would then bow reverently and quickly depart.

"What is he writing? What is inside those scrolls? Who are these angels standing in line?" I asked Wisdom.

"These are the angels sent to record every decision made by those they watch over," Wisdom answered.

"Watchers?" I asked.

"Yes, these are sent by God to record the acts and prayers of man and to bring their petitions before the Lord," Wisdom explained.

I watched an angel hand his scroll to the Recorder, who flipped through the book to the petitioner's name which contained thousands of entries of choices he had made all through his life, beginning at age five. He recorded the man's request for blessing and success in his new business venture.

The piece of paper handed to the angel had three words with check boxes next to them that read:

Petition of Man
Granted ☐
Wait ☐
Amiss ☐

MOTIVE OF THE HEART

"This man's request came from an unrepentant heart which has twisted his motives so they no longer line up with the Word of God," Wisdom explained. "Had this man repented, this request would not have been necessary. His request missed the mark and will not be granted in its present form."

There was no space on the paper for the answer "No," I noticed.

"The Lord delights in giving His children their heart's desire," Wisdom explained. "However, what is most important to man during his journey on Earth is not his possessions but the condition of his heart. A heart perfectly aligned with the will of God will receive everything it asks for. But because the Lord knows its end, a heart aligned with the path of misery and destruction will not be given anything from God but correction."

Wisdom continued, "Imagine being able to see the consequences of your child's decisions years ahead. Knowing the end from the beginning. No matter what you say to them or show them, no matter how you plead with them, they will not listen. They are determined to follow this path to its end. What would you do if, while on that path, your child asked you for a car to speed up his journey on the path of destruction? Would you not deny his request? Would it not be to keep him from harm? Your heavenly Father knows the end of each request you make to Him."

OUR TRIAL IN FAITH

I wondered about a friend who had a child die of cancer at a young age. This friend was a devout Christian, loved God, knew His Word and yet their petition for healing went unanswered. Why? I looked to Wisdom, who knew my thoughts.

"All men will face their trials of faith while on Earth and will either curse or trust God. Your question was pondered by Job and *his trial* was recorded for all men to hear the answer directly from God Himself. God used Job's trial and circumstance to teach countless men and women, down through history, the folly of leaning on the wisdom and understanding of man. Your enemy would have you curse God as he has done. For to drag a child of God to hell with him is the only way he can cause pain to Father's heart. There was great joy in heaven when Job uttered the words, 'Though He slay me, yet will I trust in Him.'"

"Why doesn't God just destroy the enemy from our planet?" I asked.

"That is your victory, my dear! God could destroy him and all fallen angels with a single word! But He will see His *children* conquer, rule and reign with Jesus for all eternity through the victory already secured on the cross. Live your life here for eternity knowing that all things will end well. All who love and follow God shall be reunited with those they love in peace and joy unspeakable, forever and ever. And at that time they will see and understand what part they played in God's perfect will."

"Some things are simply beyond our understanding and leave us with the same choice Job faced: have faith in God or curse God," I said. The necklace around my neck blinked bright white, forming another smooth jewel. "It must have something to do with the revelations I'm receiving," I said. "I wonder what the necklace will look like when all the ugly spots are filled with jewels?"

"I wonder what you will look like?" Wisdom said with a wink. "Would you like to see your entry in the Book of Life?"

I was strangely hesitant. "I'm not sure I want to see It," I said, remembering all the things I had done in my life that would bring me great shame before these Holy Ones.

The Recorder called out my name and the line of angels parted. "Ah yes, here you are. Come and see!" he commanded.

My heart raced and my knees felt weak, yet they were moving toward the Recorder and his great Book. I could look at nothing but my dirty shoes. I knew he knew everything about me and I felt so ashamed.

HOLY AND PROFANE

"Your God is a Holy God," the Recorder said, the sound waves of his voice shaking me to my core. "Do you know what 'holy' means?" he asked.

My mind raced for all sorts of possible answers: sacred, precious, of high value, regarded with great respect and reverence. But I could not find the words and said nothing.

"Holy! A standard high above even the thoughts of man, way higher than the attainment with works alone. Many have come before Him content that their good works on Earth were enough to pay for their entrance to the abode of God. Their arrogance snaps like a twig when their self-imposed blindfolds are removed and they see!" His ancient eyes locked on mine.

"Every decision, action, forsaken labor and every idle (neglected) or careless word you have ever spoken is recorded here. I have seen and recorded the works of each and every one who has spent time upon the Earth. When the books are opened and they are called to give account, not one soul will remain standing on the Day of Judgment *on his own accord.*

"Only one is worthy to enter – only one. All others enter through Him or not at all! Your name has quite a few entries you must answer for. Are you ready to give account?" he asked, looking intently at the book opened to my name.

I felt sick to my stomach and wanted to hide from their sight.

IDLE WORDS

But I say to you that for every idle word men may speak, they will give account of it in the day of judgment. For by your words you will be justified, and by your words you will be condemned.   – Matthew 12:36-37 (NKJV)

Death and life are in the power of the tongue. – Proverbs 18:21

Thou shalt also decree a thing, and it shall be established unto thee: and the light shall shine upon thy ways.   – Job 22:28

The Recorder turned the book toward me and commanded, "Look and see the works which were established by your words alone."

What I was shown forever changed the way I looked at offhanded comments, careless expressions and gossip – as well as lost opportunities to use my words for good. First of all, they are ALL recorded!

Every single time I mocked, ridiculed, or called someone a fool, it was recorded in this book under my name! Each entry also lists the effect those words had on others. The degree of harm isn't measured here, only the fact that I had contributed to the end result.

I was stunned and saddened beyond belief.

"Whether directly or indirectly, your words do not return void but accomplish what they are sent to do, my child!" Wisdom said. "Because you were created in His image, your words release a spiritual substance and authority that can heal or kill, build up or tear down. Words of gossip and ridicule carry the power to tear another child of God apart; words spoken in anger and judgment (curses) can cause sickness and death. Words of doubt and unbelief, expressed to someone else, many times cause that person to shun what the Father has in store for them."

> But I say, if you are even angry with someone, you are subject to judgment! If you call someone an idiot, you are in danger of being brought before the court. And if you curse someone, you are in danger of the fires of hell.   – Matthew 5:22 (NLT)

> It would be better for him if a millstone were hung around his neck, and he were thrown into the sea, than that he should offend one of these little ones.   – Luke 17:2 (NKJV)

> For no one can lay any foundation other than the one already laid, which is Jesus Christ. If anyone builds on this foundation using gold, silver, costly stones, wood, hay or straw, their work will be shown for what it is, because the *Day* will bring it to light. It will be revealed with fire, and the fire will test the quality of each person's work. If what has been built survives, the builder will receive a reward. If it is burned up, the builder will

suffer loss but yet will be saved – even though only as one escaping through the flames.   – 1 Corinthians 3:11-14 (NIV)

My bone clings to my skin and my flesh, and I have escaped by the skin of my teeth.   – Job 19:20 (NKJV)

"Take her to 'THE DAY,'" the Recorder ordered.

18

GREAT WHITE THRONE ROOM

At once, we stood in a great hall made of white-hot pulsating light. The doors and windows blazed with fire as did the beams and columns supporting the enormous structure. Nothing entered this room of its own accord.

In the middle were three great white thrones. I knew these three were somehow intricately interwoven with one another in a manner beyond my understanding. My focus fell upon His eyes. Fear of the "list" recorded in the Book of Life covered me with dread.

Unlike the Throne of Grace, which was peaceful and pleasant, this throne had the new arrivals on edge. Having come to the realization that their citizenship on Earth had expired, there was to be an uncertain expectancy as to what lay ahead. Their faces revealed a mixture of awe, excitement, wonder, hatred, anger, and terror. A man with enormous pride stood at the front of the line. As his name was called, he stepped forward, eager to share his brilliant conclusions as to the mystery of this event. He did not bow or show respect but stood his ground, as I somehow knew he had done his whole life on Earth. I watched as his eyes met the deeply probing eyes of the Father.

The veil of understanding was opened, and the entire life of this man appeared before us as a garden. Strewn along a well-worn path within his garden was everything he had ever done, thought of, or desired! Every hidden thing had been dug up and was laid out in plain sight for all to see. There was no such thing as a "secret" or a "mystery" here.

We stood as witnesses to the thoughts and intentions of both the man and God's heart for his life. The Father's original intent for this man's life, the missed opportunities, the forsaken assignments, along with the man's deepest desires, secrets, successes and accomplishments, all played out in perfect clarity for all to see, without a single spoken word.

The level of his understanding of the Word of God, measured much like a heat thermometer, was also revealed. The barometer of his life was just barely visible – I could "see" he had read the Bible and had even quoted Scripture, but there was no sign of his ever having spent time with the Holy Spirit. The Scriptures were filed under "nonsense" in his mind and had been taken out only to use as fuel for ridicule.

Each of us will come to this day, to our time at the front of the line, when our eyes will meet the eyes of God and we will give account for the choices we have made throughout our lives. The Father looks inside at the condition of the heart, the deep, well-worn paths most frequented by our thoughts and the fruit these thoughts have produced. I instantly understood that the thoughts and intentions of the heart produce seeds. These seeds are planted by desire. Each time they are allowed to run through the mind, they are watered and nourished and grow stronger.

Wisdom whispered, "At times, a righteous man cannot help what enters his mind, not on Earth today. It is difficult to keep a mind from seeing evil. It's what the person does with these thoughts that matters. Does he take them captive, pluck them up, and throw them out? Or does he secretly plant them in the garden of his heart? Take heed what you allow to run through your mind; its fruit in full bloom will rule you!"

You have heard that it was said, 'You shall not commit adultery'; but I say to you that everyone who looks at a woman with lust for her has already committed adultery with her in his heart.

– Matthew 5:27-28

The proud man began to speak. "I would expect to be judged on my life as a humanist," he said, "and how I treated others. If my positive actions are to be ignored and I am instead judged for using my intelligence to doubt religious doctrines created by human sinners, I would rather be eternally punished than bow to such an unfair tyrant who made it impossible for humans to succeed at this horrific game."

THE SPARK OF LIFE

A hush and stillness fell over the atmosphere as we awaited the Father's response. A single tear rolled down the face of God as He gave the command, "Return to me." The lifeless spirit within the man – in the form of a spark of light – lifted out of him and returned to the Father's heart.

I was dumbfounded at his complete lack of reverence and respect. "How could he stand before such majesty and power, so completely full of himself?" I asked Wisdom.

Wisdom's face was stern and grave as she explained, "His heart has become hard and sealed with pride. Nothing will penetrate it now. He measures himself by the standard of a fallen world with no concept of how far below heaven's requirements man has fallen."

> For the word of the cross is foolishness to those who are perishing, but to us who are being saved it is the power of God.
>
> — 1 Corinthians 1:18

"Ruled by his flesh and pride, he gave no thought to the wonder of creation and is therefore without excuse," Wisdom said sadly.

> For since the creation of the world His invisible attributes, His eternal power and divine nature, have been clearly seen, being understood through what has been made, so that they are without excuse. — Romans 1:20

We all stood and watched the fate of a fellow man unfold before us. Many times he had been presented the everlasting love of God, the gospel, and the hope of a better life on Earth and after death. Each time he mocked with scorn the believers' attempts, pronouncing them weak and profane. He was obstinate then and equally so now.

WINDOW TO HELL

Wisdom pointed to two exit gates. One was very tall, very broad, with a deep well-worn path, the other was very small and only wide enough for one to pass through at a time. "There are only two paths from here. Those whose lamps are empty are drawn to the left gate. Those with lamps full of oil see clearly which Way to go."

> Enter through the narrow gate; for the gate is wide and the way is broad that leads to destruction, and there are many who enter through it. For the gate is small and the way is narrow that leads to life, and *there are few* who find it. — Matthew 7:13-14

"How the hell do I get out of here?" The proud man shouted, cursing and screaming out justification for his life choices. He pounded on the large, left gate and demanded to be let in. As the gate opened, huge tongues of fire erupted from within, snatching the proud man into their flames and silencing his screams.

Wisdom saw my terror and squeezed my hand, "All good comes from God. When you exit through that gate, all good remains with God."

> If you try to hang on to your life, you will lose it. But if you give
> up your life for my sake, you will save it.   – Luke 9:24 (NLT)

I fell on my knees, thanking God for His provision. The voice of my spirit within rang loud in my ears, "Fear the Lord, have great reverence and respect for Him, obey His commandments, love your brother as yourself. Lay down your life at the feet of Jesus to do as He pleases. You will never be sorry, not here nor in all eternity."

Wisdom's kind, loving voice gently explained, "You see, He doesn't sit on His throne laughing as one of His children enters that horrible gate of hell. He grieves; He suffers great loss. The Laws of Eternal Justice must be upheld, even at the cost of great and terrible loss. The Way of escape has been provided. Watch and see."

I heard my name called to the throne. I saw myself step forward to the front of the line and merged with the vision. I heard my full name called, along with "daughter of Thomas E. Ross, son of Harold Ross, son of John Ross," and so on—a string of other male names which I knew to be my ancestors, dating back to the beginning of time. I stared at the crystal floor.

Then I heard His voice call my name. Looking up into the eyes of God was difficult, for I was covered in shame. When you stand in the presence of holiness, everything that is unclean or unholy manifests itself with crystal clarity in your mind. Everything in me wanted to duck for cover, run, and hide. I felt like dung before perfection, and the feeling was growing stronger by the second. I slowly looked up and locked eyes with the Creator of life itself. Everything in the room disappeared, and I became lost in the fierce beauty and power. My thoughts began to roar through my mind. Had I repented enough? Had I accepted Jesus? Did I give enough? Did I love enough? Did I do enough for the Lord? Was I going to hell? My strength left me, and I felt my knees buckle.

As if to catch my fall, the fire in God's eyes left His and entered into my eyes. A probe, so to speak, filled every vein, every organ, every nerve-ending as it made its way through my body. It penetrated my soul, flowing like a river through my mind, will, and emotions, taking inventory of all that was there and all that was missing. Just like with the man before me, all that God was seeing within me was displayed on the dome ceiling for all to see. Sins I had committed, omissions, careless words spoken, people I had passed by, uncaringly ignoring their need, began to display for all of heaven, until …

The probe passed through my soul into the cavity of my spirit. The burning light of the gaze of God found within me a reborn, quickened spirit, full of the Light, Life, and Love of His Son – the only kind of spirit able to enter heaven. God's Fire merged with my spirit, and the dome screen turned crimson red, and all my sins disappeared from the dome screen and from the minds and hearts of all looking on. They were just gone, as if they had never happened.

God's Spirit had found the life of His Son within my being and I was declared innocent and pure. I heard a roar of cheers erupt in the room as the crimson red dome turned to a brilliant white and gold color. Wisdom whispered, "This is the color of Salvation's victory!

Do you see what Jesus has done for you?" I wept in relief, in love, in deep appreciation and awe of the power and love of God Almighty, and His Son, Jesus my Savior, and His wonderful Spirit. I had passed through the eternal fire where all unworthy works – good and evil – are burned up, and what remains is the righteousness of God's Son, Jesus the Christ.

19

THE SPIRIT OF THE FEAR OF THE LORD
– πείθω –

πείθω — **convince, persuade, talk into, determine**

"Well done," I heard an unfamiliar voice say behind me. I was now in a courthouse similar to those on Earth. Standing behind the "defendant's table" was a two-foot-tall angel who had an immaculate, intricately braided beard that hung down to his stomach. He held a large book in his hand, which he flipped open and began writing in as he addressed me further. "You will need to check back often to ensure the throne of your heart is occupied by Him and that you are in proper alignment," he said firmly.

"Who are you, sir?" I asked.

"I represent the Fear of the Lord," he answered. I waited for him to expound, but he just continued to scribble away in his book.

"What do you mean, you represent the Fear of the Lord?" I asked. "Are you like an attorney?" I asked, still weak and trembling from my earlier experience. He helped me to my feet.

"You could say that, yes. I work with Counsel quite a bit," he tore a piece of paper from his book and laid it along with a pencil on the desk.

"What kind of court is this?" I asked.

He pointed to the big, round plaque above the judge's seat. The words were in Greek: – πείθω.

"What does it mean?" I asked, but he had gone. I picked up the paper, expecting to find the answer to my question, but it was blank. So I took the pencil and wrote the Greek word down, folded the paper, and put it in my pocket. I decided I would ask Wisdom what it meant.

THE GLORY

"Watch and see the answer to your question," I heard Wisdom say. The scene changed and I was standing in the throne room in heaven; Jesus sat upon a beautiful throne made of white marble. Standing before Him were thousands of angelic beings.

Upon close examination of these magnificent angels, I saw that each had a distinct personality, purpose, skill, and demeanor. I followed Jesus, who walked through the line as a general walks amongst his troops. He knew each one intimately, and I knew He had handpicked them for this mission. As His eyes met theirs, they would bow, bending to one knee in complete submission to the Lord they loved. They loved! Angels love. "Wow," I thought. "It's amazing how we paint such a shallow picture of these beings, and yet how complex, intelligent, and unique they are."

"These, too, have free will to serve God, self, or idol," Wisdom said. The love for the Lord that was in her eyes, and in the eyes of all the angels, was intoxicating. I stood behind the Lord and looked into the eyes of the angel He was speaking with. I felt drawn inside the angel's gaze.

Angels don't have tiny, black irises in their eyes, only this amazing pinwheel of intricate design as our eyes have, but with a small circle of pure white in the center. "Were our eyes like that before the fall?" I wondered. "Did our pupils turn black when they were opened to the knowledge of good and evil?"

Fine streams of liquid gold dust began flowing out of the angels' eyes, draping the Lord in glory. Wisdom's eyes read mine. "Pure. Their love and worship, it is pure. What you see is an exchange that takes place between angels and their Maker."

"Is it liquid gold?" I asked.

Wisdom smiled and said, "It is glory, given to the only One it properly belongs to, Jesus Himself. This is the substance coveted by your enemy and mine: Lucifer, light-bearer, carrier of the light or glory. He was to raise the praise and direct and carry the resulting glory to the throne of God. But he took it upon himself and would not deliver it to the One to whom it belongs. He stole it and adorned himself with it until he could no longer bear to see himself without it. This is the most sought-after substance in the kingdom of darkness and upon the Earth, and it is the product of worship. The worship you are observing releases a substance in the Spirit of Glory upon whomever it is directed. No man or angel can touch the glory that belongs to God alone and live in peace. Come, I'll show you."

THE DAWN OF MAN

We stood on a high mountain overlooking the Garden of Eden, below where God walked in the cool of the day with Adam and Eve. Perched on the cliff was Lucifer, whose appearance was that of a huge, black, bony bat. Beside him stood Michael, the archangel. Both gazed intently at the newly-formed creation below.

Lucifer's focus and intelligence were tangible. Lost in thought, he addressed Michael, his words tender. "Look how He loves them, dotes on them," Lucifer said. "How joyfully He provides for them, protects them, teaches and guides them! Their beauty and innocence are undeniable! Little versions of Himself …" His eyes narrowed and filled with fury "… who carry more power and destiny in their being than all of our forces combined! You would serve them?" he asked Michael, with disgust and seething hatred.

Michael stood firm, "I will."

"They are clothed in His glory! They wear it as a garment! How does that differ from me?" Lucifer demanded.

"You took His glory upon yourself. They have been given it from Most High! That is the difference," Michael answered.

"Michael," Lucifer begged, "I know firsthand the power and pull of that glorious garment. No one who puts it on for but a moment can ever live without it! Look at my angels, I draped the Most High's cloak of praise upon each one of them; they momentarily tasted of its pleasure and since then not one has left my side! They will not cease to war against Him until they have it for themselves."

"Have you gazed upon the consequence of your choice? Try as you may to avoid your own reflection, Lucifer, even your own glory has passed away." Michael said with disdain.

Lucifer's rage erupted and he pounced on Michael. "These 'little-gods' of His will not be satisfied with their own glory. They will covet more and more of it as well! He would have them rule over us? Never! I will take that glory from them and they will bow before me!"

Michael threw Lucifer to the ground, pinning him under his sword. "Your time is short, Lucifer, hell's fire hungers for your arrival!"

Lucifer laughed, "I'll not enter hell alone. These pitiful creatures of His will fall under my spell, Michael! They are no match for my powers of persuasion, and you know it! Lest you forget, righteousness and justice are the foundation of His throne! He judges me –- He likewise must judge them with the same measure! Will the 'heavenly Father' burn His own children?" Lucifer mocked, "He throws me into the fire, and by the law of justice He'll have to burn His pitiful children, too!" Lucifer screamed with glee. "I'm betting He won't do it! And if He doesn't condemn them as well, His throne will crumble! You see, I've got nothing to worry about, sport, nothing at all. But you do, don't you?!"

Michael was visibly shaken by the revelation of Lucifer's plan. "Depart from me, I'll not hear another word from you!"

Lucifer leapt to his feet, grinning, then dusted himself off and disappeared into the mist. Michael looked down upon the garden with great concern.

Wisdom said, "Hell was never intended for man. Your heavenly Father does not send them to hell, they choose it for themselves. He has provided a way of escape and has proven His love with the sacrifice of His own Son. What more could one ask of Him?"

I fell on my knees and wept. Oh, how many times I had touched and taken the glory in the form of "credit" for myself. Oh, how many times I had given that glory, that worship, to an idol. I'm so sorry, Lord. Scenes of idolatry upon the Earth flashed through my mind. Teenagers screaming for rock stars. Men and women worshiping the ground their spouses walk on. Idolatry in the eyes of those with ambition for that most coveted position or paycheck or place of power. "I deserve the credit!" rang through my ears, as that most powerful feeling coursed through my veins, enveloping my entire body and filling my stomach with anger and hatred.

My eyes snapped open, and standing before me was a woman dressed in flowing green attire. She held a jeweled dagger in both hands. Her eyes were a piercing green, full of hatred and power.

"They don't deserve the credit, but you do!" Her voice was soft and comforting. "You worked so hard, and they show no appreciation!"

The anger inside my heart grew stronger with each of her words. The faces of those I accused in my soul appeared before me.

"Yes, that's it; they are the cause of all your misery. They ruined your life. Look at them, full of the praise that belongs to you! You deserved that honor, you've been robbed, taken advantage of, mocked and ridiculed." I wanted to scream. She extended the dagger to me. I took it in my hands and gripped it hard. "Go ahead, kill them," she said, her eyes ablaze with charismatic lust and hatred.

"No!" I heard myself say faintly. I paused.

"It's not the Way. Don't go there," said a still, small voice within me. Yet the feelings of rebellion and anger remained strong in my soul.

"A battle is raging inside you between your soul and your spirit," Wisdom said. "You must choose your course—your spirit's humility or your soul's pride. Without a resurrected spirit and assistance from the Holy Spirit of God, a man is not able to stand against these wiles of Lucifer. For this reason, the Son was given, to atone for and empower His children to stand. Oh, that precious, precious blood of Christ!"

I threw the dagger down, and the woman in green disappeared.

"Who was that woman, Wisdom?" I asked.

"Jealousy is her name, envy is her dagger. She is a chief companion of Lucifer and enters each of his comrades. Her hold over her victims can only be broken by the power given to you by Jesus on the cross. You see, He demonstrated the way of victory over her by laying down His life and His rights for you. 'No greater love is this than a man lay down his life for his friends.'"

The experience had left me utterly exhausted. I fell into Wisdom's warm embrace and squeezed my eyes shut. She held me tight and hummed the most beautiful melody. My necklace burned and glowed once again.

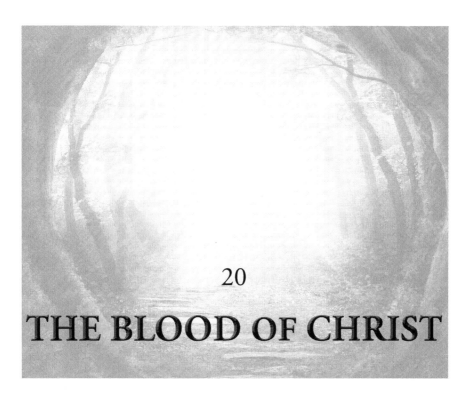

20
THE BLOOD OF CHRIST

Therefore let us draw near with confidence to the throne of grace, so that we may receive mercy and find grace to help in time of need.   – Hebrews 4:16

"Jariel, I must revisit the Throne of Grace today!" I called out.

Jariel appeared and extended his hand, "At your service!"

"It's good to see you, my friend!" I said.

"Yes, as always. You are 'ready' this time?" he asked ever so politely.

"Just need to grab my list," I said, running up the stairs.

"Another long one you crafted, I suppose?" he asked.

I bounded down the stairs, excited as a school girl, "Just one this time, Jariel, just one," I answered with a smile.

"Shall we go? Jariel asked, extending his hand.

We popped back into the same waiting room. I looked around at the others, easily spotting fidgety first-timers, smiling as I remembered the excitement mixed with fear at my last visit. I wondered how many questions they each had, but I knew not to ask.

My name was soon called and I quickly made my way through that door onto the beautiful red carpet that led to the throne room. This time there was no line, no one was on the carpet. I looked ahead and saw the two guards standing at the door in the distance.

"Is it closed?" I asked Jariel.

"What do you mean, closed?" Jariel asked, puzzled.

"Is He accepting visitors today? Where is everyone?" I asked.

"He awaits you," Jariel answered.

"No one but me today? Are you sure?" I asked a bit nervously.

"Yes, let us go," Jariel urged.

As we walked down the massive hallway, my eyes were riveted on the red carpet. I'd never seen anything like it. Was it wet or just spongy or made of some material not known to us on Earth?

"Child of God! Child of God approaches! Open the Way," one of the three-hundred-foot tall guards yelled. I turned around to see who they were talking about. No one was there, just me and my angel.

"Approach boldly," Jariel nudged.

I tried to stand erect and act confident and bold as he directed, but somehow knew that wasn't what he meant. There was nothing in me to support a bold stance. "There isn't a sliver of boldness in my bones right now, Jariel!" I said faintly.

"The boldness I speak of is not formed within your own experience. The boldness lies in the knowledge of what your feet tread upon!" Jariel sternly replied.

My necklace burned, and cracked open revealing a perfect, multicolored jewel which shined brightly upon my neck. My old filthy garments were instantly replaced by a spotless white gown.

I now knew exactly what he meant. I knelt down and touched the carpet with my hand. It was wet. It was blood. His blood, the precious Blood of Christ, paved the path to the Throne of Grace.

"There is no other way you may enter this throne room but by His blood, no other way," the guard explained.

The full revelation completely unraveled me. Deep, deep sobs erupted from my soul of the realization that I was walking upon the blood of the One I loved more than life itself. It was His blood! Freely given for this purpose, to clothe us in His perfection and to open these doors wide for all who would come. Oh, how I loved Him! I stood up and ran into the throne room, knowing without a doubt that such a sacrifice as this should never ever be doubted or debased.

"Abba, Father, Daddy!" I cried as I ran boldly across that carpet and leapt into the waiting open arms of my Father in heaven! There were no words that could express my deep love and gratitude, but I knew He knew. Buried in His loving arms, I wanted nothing from Him but Him. His presence was all I desired, and my heart yearned to serve Him.

My one and only question that visit was and is to this day, "What may I do for You today, my sweet Lord?"

The Father examined the glowing necklace around my neck. "I see you are ready for more adventures. This was only the beginning child, only the beginning," the Father said with a smile.

STAY TUNED FOR VOLUME 2
– COMING SOON –

My friend, if you know Him, please talk to Him more, meet with Him, spend time with Him. He so yearns to see and hear from you – it is what you were created for.

If you have never met Jesus but would like to, simply say this prayer and know it's a done deal.

"Jesus, I invite You to come into my heart right now and teach me who You are and who I am to You."

It is that simple. If you open your heart to the Son of God, please know with certainty, He will come in. He's been waiting for you for a long time, and once you discover how much He loves and believes in you, you'll never want to leave. He is the only One who promised, "I will never leave or forsake you." And He never will.

See you in the Throne Room of Grace!

With much love,

Shirley Seger

Sacred Secrets is available at:

store@xpmedia.com

and at Amazon.com

Printed in Great Britain
by Amazon